A Tibetan Buddhist Companion

A Tibetan Buddhist Companion

Compiled and translated by
ERIK PEMA KUNSANG

EDITED BY
Marcia Binder Schmidt
& Michael Tweed

SHAMBHALA
Boston & London
2003

Shambhala Publications, inc.
Horticultural Hall
300 Massachusetts Avenue
Boston, Massachusetts 02115
www.shambhala.com

Ornaments used throughout courtesy of Robert Beer.

9 8 7 6 5 4 3 2 1

FIRST EDITION

Printed in the United States of America
⊚ This edition is printed on acid-free paper that meets
the American National Standards Institute z39.48 Standard.
Distributed in the United States by Random House, Inc.,
and in Canada by Random House of Canada Ltd

Library of Congress Cataloging-in-Publication Data
A tibetan buddhist companion: compiled and translated by Erik Pema
Kunsang/edited by Marcia Binder Schmidt and Michael Tweed.
p.   cm.
Includes bibliographical references.
isbn 1-57062-861-0 (alk. paper)
1. Buddhism—China—Tibet—Doctrines. 2. Buddhism—Quotations,
maxims, etc. 3. Spiritual life—Buddhism. I. Kunsang, Erik Pema.
II. Schmidt, Marcia Binder. III. Tweed, Michael.
BQ7604.T53   2003
294.3'923—dc21
2003006552

All the teachings given by the Buddha have but a single purpose: to benefit sentient beings. This benefit can be the temporary peace and happiness among gods and human beings, or it can be the lasting good of liberation and enlightenment.

—JAMGÖN KONGTRÜL THE GREAT

Contents

Preface

THE PRECIOUS TEACHINGS of Buddha Shakyamuni arrived on the Tibetan plateau in the sixth century and have survived there ever since. Under the patronage of Tibet's kings, Buddhist teachers were invited from countries near and far; of these countries, present-day India is regarded as the mother source. It is often said that the inaccessibility of Tibet, with its snowy mountain ranges, helped to secure a purity of teaching and practice up until recent times. Yet another major factor in retaining such purity is the sincerity that is embodied in the basic Buddhist principles of renunciation, *bodhichitta*, devotion, and the true view.

Many countries have been blessed by the instructions of the Awakened One, and Buddhism in its various lines of transmission is branded and categorized accordingly. Thus, people today speak of "Tibetan Buddhism," as we see on the very cover of this little book.

From the Tibetan point of view, there are as many approaches, or "vehicles," as there are different types of people, while practically speaking there are three main approaches:

Hinayana, Mahayana, and Vajrayana. It does not make sense to claim that one is higher or better than another. Most important is what an individual needs in order to progress from wherever he or she is at this very moment. The three vehicles share the perspective that allows that to happen—how to remove what hinders liberation and enlightenment, how to create the right circumstances to progress, and how to gain further experience and realization.

The common approach in each case is to identify the main culprit: our ignorance, which allows selfishness expressed in emotions and actions. The three vehicles taught by the Buddha are more precious than anything else we could possibly find or achieve in this world because on every level they provide practical and realistic tools for dealing with any situation. The knowledge of how to remove ignorance and selfishness is the most valuable gift we could receive—don't you agree? Ignorance and selfishness are the cause of so much suffering, while their opposites, wisdom and compassion, are the source of all happiness and well-being. This is the most profound meaning of healing.

If I were to choose the primary characteristic that defines Tibetan Buddhism, it would be its vast variety of approaches and levels of profundity. Tibetan Buddhist masters have emphasized that there is neither conflict nor contradiction between any of the three vehicles, and encouraged an understanding that encompasses all three vehicles. In the words of Tulku Urgyen Rinpoche, "Practice the three vehicles in the same session, on the same seat."

The following precious and practical quotes are in harmony with this perspective. They reflect the immense variety of approaches and levels of profundity that have made the tapestry of Tibetan Buddhism a deep interest and daily practice of an ever-increasing number of spiritual seekers the world over. In selecting these quotes, I have focused on unifying all the teachings into a single system. This is how most great masters understand them, as well as how I myself have been taught.

If you are interested in the plight of the Tibetans, here is a selection of valid reasons for preserving their rich cultural heritage.

If you are attracted to the beauty of Tibet, here is the landscape of their profound religion, like a range of immaculate snow mountains reflecting the sunlight of wisdom and compassion with the purity of noble intentions.

If you are looking for insight and the meaning of life, here are drops scooped up from enlightenment's inexhaustible ocean.

These quotes are true jewels, and their beauty transcends that of silver, gold, and precious gemstones. String them together on the cord of your daily life.

Let them sparkle!

Introduction

I WOULD LIKE TO INTRODUCE this selection of precious quotes as practical guidance on how to live a meaningful life. They are offered simply and clearly, in the style employed by my own Buddhist teachers.

Indulge me here.

We usually wake up in the morning from a mentally absent state, having been oblivious to our surroundings, lost in sleep and dreams. The first conscious moment is a questioning: "Where am I? Oh, yes, this is where I slept. Many hours have passed, but I feel rested now." Now habits activate us. We begin to do what we are used to doing, seeing things as before, continuing in the same tracks of old aims and pursuits. We become pleased, we become sad, we get angry, attached, upset, happy, irritated. We care, we get careless, caught up, satisfied, spaced out, fed up, interested, and uninterested. The hours fly by. We get tired, then we go to sleep again.

On and on it goes, day after day, year after year. But one day perhaps it occurs to us to ask, "What is the point of it all?

Is there any? What is life all about, anyway? Maybe Buddhism can give me something. Let me try this book."

Yes, I am talking to you. You who are sitting with this book in your hands right now. You, the pilot of your body, the surfer on this wave we call life, the rider of the horse of thoughts and emotions, plans and memories. It is time to take charge of your own life. It is time to get on the beam with life, to face reality.

We do not have to carry on chasing the illusive water of a mirage. We can put some meaning into our lives. We can drink from the clear mountain stream of pithy advice from enlightened masters. The Buddha and many great masters accomplished everything there was to accomplish. They gave advice so that others might be happy, free, enlightened. These teachings come from the Buddha, and they have been passed down to us through an unbroken lineage of practitioners—they are truly tried and proven. Let me offer you a few examples.

The very moment you wake up, begin the day with a noble thought. You can find quite a few here. The noblest thought of all is called bodhichitta: "May all living beings be happy. May they not suffer. How wonderful it would be if they could find permanent happiness. May everyone attain liberation. May I help other beings reach enlightenment."

How does that feel? Isn't it true that when we care for others, selfishness and worry melt away—like frost when touched by the sun's warming rays?

What a beautiful way to start the day! You deserve a tea or coffee now.

There is always time for a little training session before

work or school. Even five or ten minutes can be used in a way that will engender tremendous benefit. Three points need to be included: beginning, middle, and end.

Begin with bodhichitta, the good heart. Gradually, as you appreciate this attitude more and more, you can include taking refuge. Refuge and bodhichitta are the excellent beginning; they give the right orientation. Imagine that there is a long line of people. They all have noble hearts, they all care for others, and they are wise and capable. In forming the noble attitude of bodhichitta, we have now taken a step forward and joined that line. We belong to the Buddha's party. How does that feel?

Now it is time for the session. There is a long day ahead. There will be ups and downs and challenges. Some levelheadedness will be required. Now is a good time to stay put. For the next little while there is absolutely nothing we need to do—just sit. It *is* possible to remain calm. It is also possible to see clearly, and it is possible to remain unswayed, yet alert and caring. We *can* hold our ground, yet be responsive and kind.

If it is possible right now, while simply sitting, it is also possible at any other moment of the day. This book includes quite a few quotes on how to simply be. That was the excellent middle.

Finally we have arrived at the excellent end. Again make a noble wish: "May the goodness of this session help all others. Just as practitioners in the past reached enlightenment and assisted all beings, may I too try my best to follow in their footsteps."

You will find that there is an ocean of deep meaning in even a short training session with these three excellent points. This is how to make our lives meaningful. You will also find that the effect of this training stays with you throughout the day; it keeps coming back at unexpected moments. In the beginning, you do not have to do everything perfectly—just give it your best.

We *can* try our best. We *can* try not to hurt others. We can take the opportunity to be helpful. We can hold the reins that control our selfish tendencies and not let them run wild. We can also take the time to see more clearly; and yes, there is time.

At day's end, we lie down to sleep. The best way is with a noble thought, and the noblest of all is again bodhichitta.

All the quotes in this book belong within the framework of these three excellent points. May this also be the framework of our lives!

There is much to be learned from books like this, but no matter how much you read there is still much more to learn about Buddhist practice. Remember, the experience of actually diving into water is vastly more complete and delightful than reading a book on how to swim. So if after getting a taste of the Dharma you are left hungry for more, I recommend you seek out a living teacher. As many practitioners in the past have discovered, personal practical advice, received directly from someone with experience who actually knows us, is of greater benefit than all the books in the greatest library.

In my short life I've had the immense good fortune to have listened to the Buddha's teachings from many masters who hold the living tradition, each of them vital and precious, like links in a chain of pure gold. Let me mention some of the most important to me—Dilgo Khyentse Rinpoche and Tulku Urgyen Rinpoche and their heart sons Chökyi Nyima Rinpoche and Tulku Pema Wangyal—to whom I am forever indebted and grateful.

THE REASON FOR LEARNING FROM OTHERS

You must listen to teachings when you first enter the Dharma. This is in order to make the right choices by understanding samsara's flaws and the virtues of nirvana.

You must listen to teachings when trying to train your mind. This is in order to turn away from being ignorant about so many things.

You must also listen to teachings when you try to practice daily. This is in order to stabilize and gain progress in your spiritual practice.

You must also listen to teachings when you have totally freed your mindstream. This is in order to cut through any conceptual doubts.

From the very first step on the path right now, all the way until you have reached the final end, it is of vital importance to rely on someone who is better than yourself. This is in order to direct your mind toward the spiritual practice of past masters and to raise your own level of experience and realization.

Those who begin by being content with knowing "just this much" and cling to it, whatever insight it may be, will never reach the end of the path, even if they practice in solitude, and will therefore not notice any sidetrack or delusion. Other people may see you as a spiritual person, but for you personally there will be no progress.

—Longchen Rabjam

Refuge

In the Buddha, the Dharma, and the noble Sangha
I take refuge until enlightenment.
By the merit of generosity and so forth[1]
May I attain buddhahood for the welfare of all beings.

TRADITIONAL TIBETAN BUDDHIST FORMULA
FOR TAKING REFUGE

The Three Turnings of the Wheel of Dharma

In order to safeguard the beginner's mind from emotions shackled by ordinary clinging to duality, the Buddha gave detailed teachings on four noble truths that primarily show the various issues that must be adopted or avoided, the flaws and their remedies. Next he taught the Dharma wheel on the absence of characteristics (emptiness) in order to stop attachment to the remedies. Finally he gave teachings describing the basic nature—this was the Dharma wheel on fully revealing the ultimate.

LONGCHEN RABJAM

The Realistic Approach

Realize all teachings to be without contradiction.
Experience all tenets to be personal advice.

Early Kadampa masters

The Dharma

The sublime Dharma is that which can dispel all suffering and all obscurations.

JAMGÖN KONGTRÜL THE GREAT

Three Excellences

Begin your practice with the excellent preparation of bodhichitta, including both the relative and ultimate state of awakened mind. Continue your practice with the main part of development stage and completion stage, free from concepts. Conclude your practice with dedicating the merit and making aspirations for the welfare of others. By doing so you are combining all the teachings of Sutra and Tantra into a single training session. Any practice we do while possessing the three excellences is always correct, while any practice we do while lacking them is never really perfect. Never forget the excellent preparation of bodhichitta, the excellent main part beyond concepts, and the excellent conclusion of dedicating the merit.

TULKU URGYEN RINPOCHE

Bodhisattva Vow

Like the deeds of the victorious ones of the past, ॰
I will endeavor in the ultimate goal of all beings: ॰
To take across those who have not crossed and liberate
    those who have not been liberated. ॰
I will give assurance to beings and establish them in
    nirvana. ॰

PADMASAMBHAVA

Pure Ethics

The swift attainment of undisturbed meditative
     concentration
Is the result of keeping pure ethics.

BUDDHA SHAKYAMUNI,
Moon Lamp Sutra

The Three Vehicles in One Sitting

Some people regard themselves as exclusively Mahayana or Vajrayana practitioners. Others say they only follow Theravada, that they don't know anything beyond that. But talking in this way only exposes one's lack of understanding. The three vehicles are not meant to be separated at all. We can practice all of them simultaneously—in fact, we need to in order to have a solid foundation. Without really applying ourselves to the four mind-changings and taking refuge, we have no real foundation from which to connect to the Buddhist teachings. Similarly, if you want to drink tea, you need a place to put the cup. You need a table, which is the same as the foundation of the Shravaka or Hinayana teachings. You also need the cup to contain the tea, which is the Mahayana attitude. And you need the tea as well—otherwise there is nothing to drink, and you *do* need a drink. Vajrayana teachings are like the liquid poured into the cup.

In the same way, in order to become enlightened we first need to connect to the Three Jewels. Taking refuge involves entrusting ourselves; this constitutes the Hinayana teachings. After that, what is the use of being the only one who is enlightened while all our mothers roam about in samsara? That would be totally shameless. It is said that the Hinayana orientation is like the little puddle of water contained in the hoofprint of a cow, while the Mahayana attitude is as vast as the entire ocean. Everyone needs to be enlightened—not only ourselves. Third, without the very profound teachings of Vajrayana, including deity, mantra, and samadhi, there is no way we can achieve full enlightenment in this same body and lifetime. Thus, we need all three vehicles together: Hinayana, Mahayana, and Vajrayana. There is no point at all in regarding oneself as some kind of superior practitioner who doesn't need "low" or "inferior" teachings. Such an attitude would be very unrealistic.

TULKU URGYEN RINPOCHE,
Repeating the Words of the Buddha

Bodhichitta

Bodhichitta means the wish to personally awaken to complete enlightenment in order to establish all sentient beings in the state of buddhahood.

JAMGÖN KONGTRÜL THE GREAT

The First Utterance

I have discovered a nectarlike truth,
Deep, calm, and simple, lucidly awake and unformed.
Whomever I explain it to, no one will understand;
So I will remain silent in the jungle.

ONE OF THE FIRST PROCLAMATIONS OF BUDDHA
SHAKYAMUNI AFTER FULLY AWAKENING TO
ENLIGHTENMENT

Ground, Path, and Fruition

The basic ground is our buddha nature, the dharmakaya of all the buddhas that is present in every sentient being. It is compared to pure, undefiled gold endowed with supreme qualities and free from any defects. How is the buddha nature present in everyone? The example given is that of oil in a mustard seed. When pressed, a mustard seed always yields oil. In the same way, in all sentient beings there is the essence of buddhahood, the buddha nature. No one lacks it. All the buddhas and bodhisattvas have buddha nature, as do all sentient beings down to the tiniest insect, without any difference whatsoever in size or quality.

The buddha nature encompasses all of samsara and nirvana. Space is beyond center and edge. Wherever space pervades, there are sentient beings. Wherever there are sentient beings, buddha nature is present. That is what is meant by the statement that buddha nature encompasses all of samsara and nirvana, all worlds, all beings.

Although buddha nature is present in everyone, we fail to recognize it. This ignorance is the main cause for wandering in samsara. Due to the ignorance of not knowing their own nature, sentient beings have strayed into confusion, like pure gold that has fallen into the mud and is temporarily defiled. Buddhas did not stray into confusion but retained their "natural seat." The difference between buddhas and sentient beings is the difference between knowing and not knowing our innate nature.

Although gold is gold, when it falls in the mud it gets covered by dirt and becomes unrecognizable. Gold temporarily covered by mud is the analogy for sentient beings who fail to recognize their own nature. All sentient beings are buddhas, but due to temporary obscurations they do not realize it. The ground is likened to pure gold, while the path is like gold that has fallen in the dirt and is covered by defilements. In this context, the path means the state of confusion.

Buddhahood, the realized state of all awakened beings, means not straying onto the path of confusion but recognizing the state of the ground as being pure gold. Due to the power of confusion, we have now strayed into the state of the path—the pure gold is temporarily covered by mud. We are temporarily under the power of confusion. Because of the sleep of ignorance, we go through the dreams of the three realms, taking rebirth among the six classes of sentient beings again and again, endlessly.

TULKU URGYEN RINPOCHE

The Four Seals That Mark the Teachings
of the Awakened Ones

Everything conditioned is impermanent.
All tainted states are painful.*
All phenomena are empty and devoid of self-entity.
Nirvana is peace.

BUDDHA SHAKYAMUNI, ON HOW FUTURE
FOLLOWERS SHOULD RECOGNIZE THE MARK OF
HIS TEACHINGS

---

* "Tainted states" means the experience of blindly clinging to the idea of
a personal identity, a "me," which is the basis of all negative emotions.

Impermanence

Gathering ends in depletion.
Rising ends in falling.
Meeting ends in parting.
Living ends in death.

FROM THE *Udana Varga,* AN EARLY
BUDDHIST SCRIPTURE

Mortality

It makes no sense to casually think,
"Today I will not die."
There is no doubt the day will come
When you too will be gone.

SHANTIDEVA

The Four Mind-Changings

This support (the precious human body) that is fully endowed with the freedoms and riches is extremely difficult to
achieve whether you reflect on its causes, identity, quantity,
or analogies. At this time, when you have achieved such a
consequential find, you must practice nothing but the sacred
Dharma, whose goal is permanent happiness.

This achievement, however, will not last for long. It
changes from moment to moment like a flash of lightning in
the sky, and, like a water bubble, there is no certainty as to
when it will disappear or when it will change. Since circumstances arise suddenly, you do not have even a hair-tip's
worth of confidence that you will not die tonight. Therefore,
do not let your Dharma practice be delayed but resolve to
practice from this very moment.

At the time of death, needless to say, food and wealth,
luxuries, family and friends, authority and so forth, even this
body of yours will be left behind. When you depart, which
happens as easily as a hair is pulled out of butter, you are accompanied only by your karma. You cannot cast away the
misdeeds you have done, and you cannot bring along virtuous deeds that you yourself did not do. The karmic deeds
you have committed are not expended, and what you have
not done you will not reap, so, without personal power but
directed by the power of your karmic deeds, you will take re-

birth into one of the higher or lower places in samsara.

What will you do if you are reborn in the three lower realms? You have no assurance that you will not take birth there. From now on, do not commit any misdeeds even at the cost of your life, and persevere in training in what is virtuous. Reflecting in this way, form the resolve "I will unmistakenly practice the Dharma of adopting and avoiding causes and effects, so that there is definite benefit for future lives!"

There is no place in samsara where you take birth by the power of karma that is ever beyond the three types of suffering. It is needless to mention the experiences of the beings in the lower realms; they are pitiful, and an unpleasant feeling arises just from thinking of them. But even when you are reborn among the pleasant states of existence through conditioned virtue, all that seems pleasant temporarily will change and vanish like a good dream in a night's sleep.

All of samsara's victory and defeat, joy and sorrow only alternate; nothing whatsoever endures. Pleasure and wealth, no matter how exquisite, are futile to pursue. All activities other than the sacred Dharma are therefore pointless deeds and do not transcend the wheel of misery. For these reasons, practice a teaching that is of true benefit for the future, namely, the sacred Dharma that brings deliverance from the three realms of samsara.

Reflecting in this way, invoke in your being a strong desire to renounce the three realms of samsara.

JAMGÖN MIPHAM RINPOCHE

Reality

Whether an enlightened buddha appears or does not appear,
the nature of things remains the basic nature of things.

BUDDHA SHAKYAMUNI, SUTRAS OF THE
PROFOUND MEANING[2]

Four Dharmas of Gampopa

Grant your blessings that my mind may follow the Dharma.
Grant your blessings that my Dharma practice may become
     the path.
Grant your blessings that the path may clarify confusion.
Grant your blessings that confusion may dawn as wisdom.

GAMPOPA

Learning and Practice

To practice without learning is like a cripple trying to climb
    a mountain.
To learn without practicing is like a blind man lost on a vast
    plain.

ORAL TRADITION

Learning

Unless one has trained one's mind in the topics of learning,
The omniscient state is farther away than the sky.
Considering this, the conquerors and their heirs
Have wisely advised us to study all topics of knowledge.

SAKYA PANDITA

Respecting the Dharma Teacher

Listen to teachings with single-minded faith and devotion
And never berate anyone else who does so.
To honor the one who explains the Dharma
Should be regarded as honoring the Buddha in person.

FROM THE *Kshitigarbha Sutra*

The Spiritual Friend

Friends, until you attain enlightenment, you need a
    teacher, so follow a supreme spiritual friend.
Until you realize the natural state, you need to learn,
    so listen to his instructions.

ATISHA

The Value of a True Teacher

Please realize that the method for all bodhisattvas to attain omniscient wisdom unquestionably results from following a true spiritual teacher.

MANJUSHRI, SPEAKING TO MANIBHADRA IN THE
Gandavyuha Sutra

Teachers in the Age of Strife

Due to the age of strife the masters have both qualities
    and faults.
There is no one who is continually free of any misdeed.
Therefore disciples should, after carefully examining,
Follow someone who has mostly good qualities.

PUNDARIKA, THE SECOND RIGDEN KING
OF SHAMBHALA

The Vajrayana Master and Disciple

In general, you should follow someone:
who is learned in all the sections of the Vajrayana tantras;
who can distinguish the different philosophical views;
whose being has been ripened by an uninterrupted stream of
     empowerment;
who is free from making conflicts between the samayas
     accepted in the empowerment and the vows;
whose being is peaceful and gentle due to having few
     negative emotions and thoughts;
who has comprehended the entire tantric meaning of
     ground, path, and fruition in the Secret Mantra
     Vajrayana;
who has had a vision of the yidam deity and perfected the
     signs of recitation practice;
who has freed his own being through realization of the
     natural state;
who is able to ripen the minds of others through his great
     compassion;
who has abandoned worldly activities due to having given
     up the attachment to this life;
who is focused on the Dharma with the exertion of
     accepting future lives;
whose heart is weary due to seeing the misery of samsara
     and who encourages others similarly;
who is skilled in the methods of cherishing disciples by

means of taming beings according to their needs;
and who possesses the blessings of the lineage because of
    fulfilling his guru's command.

A disciple possessing these characteristics should be
    accepted as suitable to receive teaching; someone:
who takes great delight in and is deeply interested in the
    master and his oral instructions;
who possesses enthusiastic longing and confident trust, as
    well as the perfect cause for receiving the blessing,
    which is pure trust;
who has established the resolve of a fortitude that does not
    give in to procrastination and laziness when accom-
    plishing the unexcelled;
who is able to realize easily the profound meaning of the
    natural state;
who has little attachment to the joys and riches of samsaric
    life such as food and clothing;
who is able to receive the blessings due to highly revering
    the master and the supreme deity;
who is able to engage in the profound practices by having
    resolved doubts and uncertainties about the path of
    the Secret Mantra;
who is free from ordinary distractions such as passion,
    aggression, and delusion;
who is without violations of the root and branch samayas;
who is tireless and exuberant in the practice of the pro-
    found path;
and who never violates the master's word.

Tsikey Chokling II

Mandala Offering

The earth is perfumed with scented water and strewn with
    flowers,
Adorned with Mount Meru, the four continents, the sun,
    and the moon.
Imagining this as the buddha realm, I offer it
So that all beings may enjoy that pure realm.

TRISONG DEUTSEN, THE KING OF TIBET WHO
ESTABLISHED THE BUDDHIST TEACHINGS

Taking Refuge

In the supreme among humans, all the buddhas of the ten directions, I and all the infinite sentient beings take refuge from this very moment until reaching supreme enlightenment.

In the supreme among states of peace, devoid of attachment, the Dharma teachings of the ten directions, I and all the infinite sentient beings take refuge from this very moment until reaching supreme enlightenment.

In the supreme among assemblies, the members of the noble sangha who are beyond reverting and who dwell in the ten directions, I and all infinite sentient beings take refuge from this very moment until reaching supreme enlightenment.

PADMASAMBHAVA

The Vajrayana Path

There are two kinds of accumulations: the accumulation of merit with concepts and the nonconceptual accumulation of wisdom. The accumulation of merit with concepts includes the preliminary practices, the *ngöndro*. The nonconceptual accumulation of wisdom is the abiding in the samadhi of the natural state. By gathering the two accumulations, we unfold the two types of supreme knowledge—the knowledge that perceives whatever exists and the knowledge that perceives the nature *as it is*. By unfolding the two types of supreme knowledge, we realize the two kayas, dharmakaya and rupakaya. Rupakaya means "form body" and has two aspects: sambhogakaya, which is the form of rainbow light, and nirmanakaya, which is the physical form of flesh and blood. This is a summary of the Vajrayana path.

Vajrayana is said to be a swift path to enlightenment simply because of unifying means and knowledge, development stage and completion stage. Vajrayana practice involves combining the visualization of a deity together with the recognition of mind essence; that is why it is a swift path. Vajrayana training is the means to realize that everything, *as it is*, all that appears and exists, is the buddha mandala. That is why we train in sadhana practice.

Tulku Urgyen Rinpoche

37

Preliminary Practices

Having obtained the supreme freedoms and riches, and
      being weary of impermanence, ❁
With intense renunciation endeavor in accepting and
      rejecting what concerns cause and effect. ❁
The person possessing faith and compassion ❁
Who wishes to attain the supreme and common
      accomplishments in this very life ❁
Should ripen his being through empowerment and, with
      totally pure samaya, ❁
Take refuge, the root of the path, ❁
And generate the twofold bodhichitta, the essence of the
      path. ❁
All evil deeds and obscurations, the conditions adverse to
      the arising of experiences and realizations ❁
Of Vajrayana, the ultimate part of the path, ❁
Should be purified through the profound practice of
      Vajrasattva. ❁
In order to perfect the positive conditions, the
      accumulations of merit and wisdom, ❁
Offer the mandalas of the oceanlike realms of the three
      kayas. ❁
In particular, apply the key points of the essence of all
      the paths, ❁
The guru yoga of devotion. ❁

Padmasambhava

Reducing Practice to Its Essence

Of all teachings, the ultimate is emptiness, of which compassion is the very essence. It is like a very powerful medicine, a panacea that can cure every disease in the world. And just like that very powerful medicine, realization of the truth of emptiness, the nature of reality, is the remedy for all the different negative emotions.

ATISHA

Feast Song*

On the wish-fulfilling tree of karma linked with good
    wishes,
The youthful peacock of east India has arrived.
Turn your tail parasol to face the sacred teachings
So we youngsters can also step onto the path of freedom.

In the Queen of Spring's chariot of merit,
The melodious voice of the cuckoo bird from the jungle
    of south Bhutan has arrived.
With a song sweeter than the flute of celestial maidens,
We receive the auspicious omen of a joyful
    summer season.

Vajra brothers and companions assembled here with
    harmonious karma and wishes,
Our teacher is present and has arrived at the gathering of
    Dharma.
During this feast of drinking the nectar of ripening and
    liberation,
I have the special task of singing a joyful song.

* This song is usually sung during the feast of a Vajrayana assembly.

Amid this gathering of unchanging great bliss,
We behold the countenance of the yidam and guru even
      without meditating.
So let us request the siddhi of attaining the rainbow body
      of dharmakaya,
Through the vehicle of luminous wakefulness, the heart
      essence of the mother dakinis.

JIGMEY LINGPA

Farewell to Ego-Clinging

The basis of delusion is ego-clinging, holding on to the idea of "I." Delusion is grounded in a lack of understanding of how the nature of all things is empty and insubstantial. Another basis of delusion is failing to recognize the luminous nature of things. By realizing the nonexistence of a self and releasing the tight grip of ego, we will naturally and automatically understand that all other things are empty and devoid of identity. In this way, the intermediate set of teachings are more profound than the first. It is not just the mind that is insubstantial; everything else as well is naturally empty. Not knowing that everything is naturally empty is ignorance and confusion. Similarly, compared to the second set of teachings, the perspective of the third set is more profound. Not only is everything empty and unconstructed: it is all a state of purity totally endowed with immense qualities.

When hearing what the Buddha says about how things are, we as individuals can understand something. We do get a feeling that, "Oh, yes, it is like this." We have some confidence. The Dharma, and especially the pith instructions, address exactly what is wrong and how to change it. They hit home.

We may study Buddhism. We may think about it and reflect. But, most essentially, we need to practice, to train in the great meditation of nonmeditation, as soon as possible. Do not think, "I will practice later." That attitude makes it never: our time simply runs out. Time will not wait for us. The ultimate practice is undistracted nonmeditation, which obliterates the root of confusion. It totally and permanently obliterates all karma, disturbing emotions, and habitual tendencies.

To begin with, we need some method, some techniques to lead us to the ultimate. The best method is of course effortlessness, but effortlessness cannot be taught or striven after. Even if we try—especially if we try—we can't become automatically effortless. Though effortlessness just does not seem to spontaneously take place; yet it is a fact that confused experience will fall apart the moment we simply let be in a nondualistic state. Right now, for most of us, every moment of ordinary experience is governed by conditioning. Our present habit is dominated by a deliberate effort. Therefore, we have no choice but to use our present habit of deliberate effort to arrive at effortlessness. Once we are accustomed to effortful meditation, we can make the leap to the effortless state.

CHÖKYI NYIMA RINPOCHE,
Present Fresh Wakefulness

The Vajrayana Master

Lady Tsogyal asked the Master: "Great Master, the master and teacher is of the greatest importance when entering the door of the Secret Mantra (Vajrayana) teachings. What should be the characteristics of the master whom one follows?"

The Master replied: "The master and teacher is of sole importance. The characteristics of a master are these: He should have trained his mind, he should possess many oral instructions, and he should have vast learning and experience in practice and meditation. He should be stable-minded and skilled in the methods of changing the minds of others. He should have great intelligence and care for others with compassion. He should have great faith and devotion toward the Dharma. If you follow such a master, it is like finding a wish-fulfilling jewel; all your needs and wishes will be fulfilled."

PADMASAMBHAVA, RECORDED BY YESHE TSOGYAL,
HIS CHIEF DISCIPLE

Five Ways of Sustaining the Essence

Elevate your experience and remain wide open like the sky.
Expand your mindfulness and remain pervasive like
    the earth.
Steady your attention and remain unshakable like a
    mountain.
Brighten your awareness and remain shining like a flame.
Clear your thought-free wakefulness and remain lucid
    like a crystal.

DAKPO TASHI NAMGYAL,
Clarifying the Natural State

The Yidam Deity

Lady Tsogyal asked the Master: "Why is it important to practice the yidam deity?"

The Master replied: "It is essential to practice a yidam deity because by doing so you will attain siddhis, your obstacles will be removed, you will obtain powers, receive blessings, and give rise to realization. Since all these qualities result from practicing the yidam deity, without the yidam deity you will just be an ordinary person. By practicing the yidam deity you attain the siddhis, so the yidam deity is essential."

Lady Tsogyal asked the Master: "When practicing a yidam deity, how should we meditate and practice in order to attain accomplishment?"

The Master replied: "Since means and knowledge are to practice the spontaneously present body, speech, and mind through the method of a yoga sadhana, they will be accomplished no matter how you carry out the sadhana aspects endowed with body, speech, and mind. They will be accomplished when the sadhana and recitation are practiced in a sufficient amount."

Lady Tsogyal asked the Master: "How should we approach the awakened yidam deity?"

The Master replied: "Realize that you and the yidam deity are not two and that there is no yidam deity apart from yourself. You approach the yidam deity when you realize that your nature is the state of nonarising dharmakaya."

Lady Tsogyal asked the Master: "If one's view is high, is it permissible to dispense with the yidam deity?"

The Master replied: "If you attain confidence in the correct view, then that itself is the yidam deity. Do not regard the yidam deity as a form body. Once you realize the nature of dharmakaya, you will have accomplished the yidam deity."

Lady Tsogyal asked the Master: "What should we do to have a vision of the yidam deity?"

The Master replied: "Do not regard the yidam deity as a form body; it is dharmakaya. The meditation on this form body as manifesting from dharmakaya and appearing with color, attributes, ornaments, attire, and major and minor marks should be practiced as being visible while devoid of a self-nature. It is just like the reflection of the moon in water. When you attain mental stability by practicing like this, you will have a vision of the deity, receive teachings, and so forth. If you cling to such experiences, you will go astray and be caught by Mara. Do not become fascinated or overjoyed by such visions, since they are only the manifestations of your mind."

PADMASAMBHAVA, RECORDED BY YESHE TSOGYAL,
HIS CHIEF DISCIPLE

Unity

The great Middle Way free of mental constructs
And the Great Perfection of lucid wakefulness—
There is no view superior to the fact
That these two are synonyms and mean the same.

JAMGÖN MIPHAM RINPOCHE

The Noble Heart

Just as the buddhas of former times
Formed the resolve toward enlightenment
And gradually abided by
The precepts of a bodhisattva,
So will I, for the welfare of beings,
Form the resolve toward enlightenment
And likewise gradually train
In these same precepts!

TRADITIONAL VOW OF A BODHISATTVA

Supplication to the Kagyü Lineage

Great Vajradhara, Tilo, Naro,
Marpa, Mila, Lord of Dharma Gampopa,
Knower of the Three Times, omniscient Karmapa,
Holders of the four great and eight lesser lineages—
Drigung, Taklung, Tsalpa—these three, glorious Drukpa,
    and so on,
Masters of the profound path of Mahamudra,
Incomparable protectors of beings, the Dakpo Kagyü,
I supplicate you, the Kagyü gurus.
I hold your lineage; grant your blessings so that I will
    follow your example.

Revulsion is the foot of meditation, as is taught.
To this meditator who is not attached to food and wealth,
Who cuts the ties to this life,
Grant your blessings so that I have no desire for honor and
    gain.

Devotion is the head of meditation, as is taught.
The guru opens the gate to the treasury of oral
    instructions.
To this meditator who continually supplicates him
Grant your blessings so that genuine devotion is born in me.

Awareness is the body of meditation, as is taught.
Whatever arises is fresh—the essence of realization.
To this meditator who rests simply without altering it
Grant your blessings so that my meditation is free from
 conception.

The essence of thoughts is dharmakaya, as is taught.
Nothing whatever but everything arises from it.
To this meditator who arises in unceasing play
Grant your blessings so that I realize the inseparability of
 samsara and nirvana.

Through all my births may I not be separated from the
 perfect guru
And so enjoy the splendor of Dharma.
Perfecting the virtues of the paths and bhumis,
May I speedily attain the state of Vajradhara.

PENGARWA JAMPAL SANGPO

Rejoicing

Once again the perfect Buddha said to Youthful Moonlight: "Youthful one, this being so, a bodhisattva mahasattva who aspires to achieve this samadhi, and who wishes to awaken quickly, truly, and fully to unexcelled true and complete enlightenment, should be skilled in means.

"Youthful one, how does a bodhisattva mahasattva become skilled in means? Youthful one, a bodhisattva mahasattva should keep an attitude of connectedness to all sentient beings. A bodhisattva mahasattva should thus rejoice in the good roots[3] of sentient beings and in whatever merit they may have. Three times a day and three times a night, he should rejoice in the good roots of all beings and in their accumulation of merit, and then, with the resolve aimed at the state of omniscient enlightenment, he should give away his good roots and accumulated merit to all sentient beings.

"Youthful one, by possessing the merit resulting from being skilled in means, a bodhisattva mahasattva will quickly attain this samadhi, and he will quickly awaken truly and fully to unexcelled true and complete enlightenment."

BUDDHA SHAKYAMUNI, SPEAKING
TO A DISCIPLE IN THE *King of Samadhi Sutra*

The Ten Things to Be Understood

Understand that outer appearances are unreal because they
 are illusion.

Understand that inner mind is empty because it is devoid of
 self-entity.

Understand that thoughts are momentary because they
 occur due to conditions.

Understand that both your physical body and your voice are
 impermanent because they are conditioned.

Understand that the consequences of your actions are in-
 evitable because all the pleasure and pain of sentient
 beings result from karma.

Understand that pain is your spiritual friend because it is the
 cause of renunciation.

Understand that pleasure and happiness are the demons of
 attachment because they are the roots of samsara.

Understand that many engagements are obstacles for merit
 because they hinder spiritual practice.

Understand that enemies and obstructors are your teachers
 because obstacles are inspiration for spiritual practice.

Understand that everything is of equal nature because all
 phenomena are ultimately devoid of self-nature.

These were the ten things to understand.

GAMPOPA

*Lamp Offering**

This illuminating lamp of original pure awareness
I offer to the mandala deities of knowledge holder
    Padmasambhava.
May all beings, my mothers, wherever awareness pervades,
Attain the dharmakaya level of aware emptiness.

JAMGÖN MIPHAM RINPOCHE

* A pure wish traditionally made while holding a lamp or candle to dispel the darkness of ignorance of all beings.

Fully Opened Mind

The difference between buddhas and sentient beings is like the difference between the narrowness and the openness of space. Sentient beings are like the space held within a tightly closed fist, while buddhas are fully open, all-encompassing.

TULKU URGYEN RINPOCHE

Dharmakaya

Venerable Ananda, all buddhas are the dharmakaya.
They are not the body nurtured by foodstuff.

VIMALAKIRTI,
Vimalakirti Nirdesha Sutra

The Original Pure Land

Padmasambhava is to be inseparable from the primordial
      nature.
His Copper-Colored Mountain buddhafield is the purity of
      your personal experience.
May everyone be born in this original pure land,
The uncontrived natural state of indivisible appearance and
      awareness.

CHOKGYUR LINGPA

Om Mani Padme Hung

OM MANI PADME HUNG is the quintessence of the Great Compassionate One, so the merit of uttering it just once is incalculable. The possible multiplication resulting from a single seed of the lotus flower lies beyond the reach of thought, but compared to that, the merit of uttering the Six Syllables just once is even greater.

A single sesame seed can multiply into many, but the merit of uttering the Six Syllables just once is even greater. The four great rivers and countless other minor rivers flow into the salty ocean, but the merit of uttering the Six Syllables just once is even greater. All needs and wishes are granted when you supplicate the precious wish-fulfilling jewel, but the merit of uttering the Six Syllables just once is even greater.

OM MANI PADME HUNG

It is possible to count the number of raindrops falling during twelve years of monsoon, but the merit of uttering the Six Syllables just once cannot be counted. It is possible to count all the grains sown on the four continents, but the merit of uttering the Six Syllables just once cannot be counted. It is possible to count the drops of water in the great ocean, one by one, but the merit of uttering the Six Syllables just once cannot be counted. It is possible to count each hair on the bodies of all animals in existence, but the merit of uttering the Six Syllables just once cannot be counted.

OM MANI PADME HUNG

The Six Syllables are the quintessence of the Great Compassionate One. It is possible to wear down a mountain of meteoric iron that is eighty thousand miles high by rubbing it once every eon with the softest cotton from Kashika, but the merit of uttering the Six Syllables just once cannot be exhausted. It is possible for a tiny insect to finish eating Mount Sumeru to the core, but the merit of uttering the Six Syllables just once cannot be exhausted. It is possible for the tito bird to remove the sand of River Ganges with its beak, but the merit of uttering the Six Syllables just once cannot be exhausted. It is possible for a small breeze to scatter the earth of the four continents and Mount Sumeru, but the merit of uttering the Six Syllables just once cannot be exhausted.

OM MANI PADME HUNG

It is possible to calculate the merit of creating a stupa made of the seven precious substances filled with relics of the buddhas of all the world systems and making constant offerings to it, but the merit of uttering the Six Syllables just once cannot be calculated. It is possible to calculate the amount of merit from offering incense, lamps, perfumes, cleansing water, music, and so forth to buddhas and buddha realms in a number that equals the grains of sand found in the entire world system, but the merit of uttering the Six Syllables just once cannot be calculated.

OM MANI PADME HUNG

These Six Syllables are the quintessence of the mind of noble Avalokiteshvara. If you recite them one hundred eight times a day, you will not take rebirth in the three lower realms; in your next life you will attain a human body; and in actuality you will have a vision of noble Avalokiteshvara. If, daily, you recite the mantra correctly twenty-one times, you will be intelligent and able to retain whatever you learn. You will have a melodious voice and become adept in the meaning of the entire buddhadharma. If you recite this mantra seven times daily, all your misdeeds will be purified and all your obscurations will be cleared away. In subsequent lives, no matter where you take birth, you will never be separated from noble Avalokiteshvara.

When someone is afflicted by disease or an evil influence, compared to any mundane ritual of healing or of repelling obstacles, the merit of the Six Syllables is much more effective for warding off obstacles or disease. Compared to any medical treatment or cure, the Six Syllables are the strongest remedy against sickness and evil.

The virtues of the Six Syllables are immeasurable and cannot be fully described even by the buddhas of the three times. Why is that? It is because this mantra is the quintessence of the mind of the noble bodhisattva Avalokiteshvara, who continuously watches over the six classes of sentient beings with compassion. Thus recitation of this mantra liberates all beings from samsara.

Padmasambhava

Supplication to Your Root Guru

In the dharmadhatu palace of Akanishtha
I supplicate at the feet of the root guru,
The essence of all the buddhas of the three times,
Who directly shows my mind as dharmakaya.

TRADITIONAL CHANT

Bodhisattvas

By composing their minds in equanimity, they see things correctly and exactly as they are. By seeing things correctly and exactly as they are, the bodhisattvas embrace all sentient beings with compassion.

BUDDHA SHAKYAMUNI,
Sutra of Collecting All Virtues

Seven Points of Training the Mind

Listen, noble children:

Like bubbles in water, all compounded things are
    impermanent.

Like a ripe poisonous fruit, all samsaric pleasures, though
    seemingly pleasant at the time, are actually painful.

Like chasing the water of a mirage, conditioned states are
    never-ending.

Like the good or bad experiences in a dream, all the aims of
    this life are utterly meaningless.

Like a person recovered from smallpox, the excellent
    fruition of liberation never reverts to suffering.

Like a fine staircase, a sublime master's oral instructions are
    the path for ascending to the palace of liberation.

Like a cultivated field, nonconceptual meditation is the
    basis for the growth of samadhi.

VIMALAMITRA, GREAT INDIAN MASTER OF THE
DZOGCHEN TEACHINGS

Aspiration

From the great Samantabhadra Vajradhara
Down to our kind root guru,
May the aspirations made for the benefit of beings
Be fulfilled this very day.

TRADITIONAL CHANT

Parting Advice

Since life is conditioned, it has no permanence.
Since sense objects are perceptions, they have no true
     existence.
Since the path stage is delusion, it has no reality.
Since the ground is the natural state, it has no concreteness.
Since mind is thought, it has no basis or root.
I have yet to find any "thing" that truly exists.

YESHE TSOGYAL

Bodhichitta Aspiration

May the precious mind of enlightenment
Arise in those in whom it has not arisen.
Where it has arisen, may it not wane
But increase further and further.

TRADITIONAL CHANT

The Sutra of the Heart of Transcendent Knowledge

Thus have I heard. Once the Blessed One was dwelling in Rajagriha at Vulture Peak mountain, together with a great gathering of the sangha of monks and a great gathering of the sangha of bodhisattvas. At that time, the Blessed One entered the samadhi that expresses the Dharma called "profound illumination," and at the same time noble Avalokiteshvara, the bodhisattva mahasattva, while practicing the profound prajnaparamita, saw in this way: he saw the five skandhas to be empty of nature.

Then, through the power of the Buddha, venerable Shariputra said to noble Avalokiteshvara, the bodhisattva mahasattva, "How should a son or daughter of noble family train, who wishes to practice the profound prajnaparamita?"

Addressed in this way, noble Avalokiteshvara, the bodhisattva mahasattva, said to venerable Shariputra, "O Shariputra, a son or daughter of noble family who wishes to practice the profound prajnaparamita should see in this way: seeing the five skandhas to be empty of nature. Form is emptiness; emptiness also is form. Emptiness is no other than form; form is no other than emptiness. In the same way, feeling, perception, formation, and consciousness are emptiness. Thus, Shariputra, all dharmas are emptiness. There are no characteristics. There is no birth and no cessation. There is no impurity and no purity. There is no decrease and no increase.

Therefore, Shariputra, in emptiness there is no form, no feeling, no perception, no formation, no consciousness; no eye, no ear, no nose, no tongue, no body, no mind; no appearance, no sound, no smell, no taste, no touch, no dharmas; no eye dhatu up to no mind dhatu, no dhatu of dharmas, no mind consciousness dhatu; no ignorance, no end of ignorance up to no old age and death, no end of old age and death; no suffering, no origin of suffering, no cessation of suffering, no path, no wisdom, no attainment, and no nonattainment. Therefore, Shariputra, since the bodhisattvas have no attainment, they abide by means of prajnaparamita. Since there is no obscuration of mind, there is no fear. They transcend falsity and attain complete nirvana. All the buddhas of the three times, by means of prajnaparamita, fully awaken to unsurpassable, true, complete enlightenment. Therefore, the great mantra of prajnaparamita, the mantra of great insight, the unsurpassed mantra, the unequaled mantra, the mantra that calms all suffering should be known as truth, since there is no deception. The prajnaparamita mantra is said in this way:

OM GATE GATE PARAGATE PARASAMGATE BODHI SVAHA

Thus, Shariputra, the bodhisattva mahasattva should train in the profound prajnaparamita."

Then the Blessed One arose from that samadhi and praised noble Avalokiteshvara, the bodhisattva mahasattva, saying, "Good, good, O son of noble family; thus it is, O son of noble family, thus it is. One should practice the profound prajnaparamita just as you have taught and all the tathagatas will rejoice."

When the Blessed One had said this, venerable Shariputra and noble Avalokiteshvara, the bodhisattva mahasattva, that whole assembly and the world, with its gods, humans, asuras, and gandharvas, rejoiced and praised the words of the Blessed One.

PRAJNAPARAMITA LITERATURE

Aspiration for the Vajra Master and the Practice Lineage

May the life of the eminent guide last for one hundred eons,
May the Dharma tones of the true meaning resound to the
    ends of the world,
May the tradition of the Practice Lineage ripen like crops
    at autumn,
And may an auspicious golden age unfold with virtuous
    goodness.

JIGDREL YESHE DORJE, DUDJOM RINPOCHE

Enlightened Essence

For example, just as butter is present in milk, the enlightened
essence is present in all sentient beings.

BUDDHA SHAKYAMUNI,
Mahanirvana Sutra

Request for the Teacher to Remain As the Vajra Body, Speech, and Mind

OM AMARANI JIVANTIYE SVAHA

Your indestructible vajra body of great bliss, visible and yet
empty,
Fully adorned with the youthfulness of the major and
minor marks,
Is the marvelous embodiment of the victorious ones, a nirmanakaya to teach beings.
May your life be firm as the unchanging vajra body.

Your unobstructed vajra speech, audible and yet empty,
Voice of the profound and secret teachings, endowed with
sixty qualities,
Is the sambhogakaya manifested to accord with the
inclination of beings.
May your life be firm as the unceasing vajra speech.

Your vajra mind beyond arising, dwelling, and ceasing,
cognizant and yet empty,
Profound and luminous wakefulness, the sphere from which
all things arise,
Is the all-pervasive lord, the dharmakaya essence of the
victorious ones.
May your life be firm as the unmistaken vajra mind.

Sun of buddha activity in the all-pervading sky,
Radiating welfare and happiness beyond rising and
    setting,
Eminent sustainer who makes the lotus garden of the
    teachings and beings bloom,
May you shine for an ocean of eons.

TERDAG LINGPA GYURME DORJE

Dependent Origination

What is meant by dependent origination? It means that nothing included within inner or outer phenomena has arisen without a cause. Neither have they originated from what are not their causes; that is, noncauses such as a permanent creator [in the form of] the self, time, or the Almighty. The fact that phenomena arise based on the interdependence of their respective causes and conditions coming together is called dependent origination. To proclaim this is the unique approach of the Buddha's teaching.

In this way, the arising of all outer and inner phenomena require that their respective causes and conditions come together in the appropriate manner. When these factors are incomplete, phenomena do not arise, while when complete, they will definitely arise. That is the nature of dependent origination.

Thus, dependent origination ranks as an essential and profound teaching among the treasuries of the Buddha's words. The one who perceives dependent origination with the eyes of discriminating knowledge will come to see the qualities that have the nature of the eightfold noble path, and with the wisdom gaze that comprehends all objects of knowledge will perceive the dharmakaya of buddhahood. Thus it has been taught.

JAMGÖN MIPHAM RINPOCHE,
Gateway to Knowledge, Volume 1

Between Two Thoughts

In the gap between two thoughts,
Thought-free wakefulness manifests unceasingly.

MILAREPA

Shri Singha's Song

I am the Shri Singha
Who has mastered wakeful awareness.
Through the expansive vastness of wide-open equality,
This wisdom essence is utterly free.

SHRI SINGHA,
Wellsprings of Perfection

The Three Types

Know that there are three types of people:
Inferior, mediocre, and superior.

The inferior are said to be those
Who by any of the various means
Strive for their own benefit
To merely attain the pleasures of samsara.

The mediocre are said to be those
Who turn their back on samsara's pleasures
And also refrain from evil deeds,
Yet merely pursue a personal peace.

The superior are said to be those
Who through understanding their own suffering
Deeply desire to completely end
The sufferings of all other beings.

ATISHA

Chö: Cutting

Chö is the tradition of letting go. It is to relinquish selfishness and is an eminent method to abandon attachment, to be free. Cutting, the meaning of chö practice, is cutting through subject-object fixation, cutting through dualistic experience. This teaching from the female teacher Machig Labdrön was the only one that was translated from Tibetan into the Indian languages. That is how special it is. Chö is practiced out of the unity of emptiness and compassion. In this courageous compassion there is no hesitation, no doubt in acting for the welfare of beings.

TULKU URGYEN RINPOCHE

The Essence of Chö

Compared to begging one hundred times, "Save me,
    protect me!"
It is much more effective to say once, "Devour me!"

MACHIG LABDRÖN

Buddhist Principles

Do not commit any evil;
Do what is perfectly good;
Fully tame your own mind.
That is the teaching of the Buddha.

TRADITIONAL TEACHING

Ripening and Liberating

The mind essence of sentient beings is the luminous
   nature of self-awareness,
The unfabricated awakened state, a continuity that is
   spontaneously present.
Once you embark on the path of ripening and liberating
   this luminous nature,
You clearly perceive the fruition within your own being.

FROM THE *Subsequent Tantra of the Bathing Elephant*

Four Types of Teacher

The outer teacher is the preceptor, who imparts the vows
 of individual liberation.
The inner teacher is the spiritual guide, who has the
 bodhichitta resolve for enlightenment.
The secret teacher is the vajra master, who matures the
 wisdom of Vajrayana empowerment.
The ultimate teacher is the root guru, who points out the
 definitive meaning, the natural state of the Great
 Perfection.

These are the four great mentors, through the beginning,
 middle, and end.

TSIKEY CHOKLING II

The Aspiration of Buddha Samantabhadra

Ho!
Everything—appearance and existence, samsara and
  nirvana—
Has a single ground, yet two paths and two fruitions,
And magically displays as awareness or unawareness.

Through Samantabhadra's prayer, may all beings become
  buddhas,
Completely perfected in the abode of the dharmadhatu.

The ground of all is uncompounded,
And the self-arising great expanse, beyond expression,
Has neither the name "samsara" nor "nirvana."

Realizing just this, you are a buddha;
Not realizing this, you are a being wandering in samsara.

I pray that all you beings of the three realms
May realize the true meaning of the inexpressible
  ground.

BUDDHA SAMANTABHADRA,
The Tantra That Directly Reveals Samantabhadra's Mind,
INCLUDED IN A COLLECTION OF TERMA TREASURES
CONCEALED BY PADMASAMBHAVA TO BE
REVEALED MANY CENTURIES LATER

Pilgrimage

Previously, enlightened beings, bodhisattvas, and great siddhas would bestow blessings on a place where they stayed due to their realization. In this dark age, it is somewhat reversed: the place now has to bless the people. The lamas of Tibet show delight and joy when they come to such a sacred place.

TULKU URGYEN RINPOCHE

Four Pilgrimage Places of the Buddha

Virtuous ones, after my passing, devoted sons and daughters of noble character should visit and remember these four places for as long as they live.

Which four? Here the Buddha was born. Here the Buddha awakened to true and complete enlightenment. Here the Buddha turned the twelvefold wheels of the Dharma. Here the Buddha passed completely beyond suffering.

Virtuous ones, after my passing, there will be people who circumambulate the stupas and there will be people who bow down before them. It is for such people that these words are spoken.

BUDDHA SHAKYAMUNI,
Minor Vinaya Precepts

Helping Anyone in Distress

While proclaiming her great vows, Queen Shrimala said to the Buddha: "World-Honored One, from now until I attain enlightenment, if I see any sentient beings bereft of parents or children, imprisoned, sick, distressed, or suffering from any kind of danger or misfortune, I will not forsake them. Instead, I will give them peace and security, help them properly, and relieve them of all their sufferings."

FROM THE *Sutra of the True Lion's Roar of Queen Shrimala*

Sukhavati

Ananda,* the sentient beings who bring to mind Buddha Amitabha's countenance, who create a boundless number of virtuous roots, who dedicate them with the resolve set upon supreme enlightenment, and in this way make the aspiration to be born in that realm, will, on the verge of death, behold before them Buddha Amitabha, the Thus Gone, the Foe Destroyer, the truly and completely awakened one, encircled by a multitude of spiritual practitioners. Having beheld blessed Amitabha, they will pass on in a joyful frame of mind and take rebirth in the blissful realm of Sukhavati.†

BUDDHA SHAKYAMUNI,
Amitabha Sutra DESCRIBING THE FOUR CAUSES FOR
REBIRTH IN THAT BUDDHAFIELD

---

* Ananda was the Buddha's chief disciple.
† Sukhavati is the pure realm of Buddha Amitabha, praised by all buddhas as the easiest realm outside samsara in which to take rebirth.

Song of Naropa

This mind that knows emptiness
Is itself the awakened mind, bodhichitta.
The buddha potential is just this.
The sugata essence is just this.

Because of tasting what is,
It is also the great bliss.
The understanding of Secret Mantra is just this.
Means and knowledge are just this.

The vast and profound is just this.
Samantabhadra and consort are just this.
This space and wisdom, perceiving while being empty,
Are what is called "knowing original enlightenment."

This self-knowing, though one is still deluded,
Does not depend on other things,
So self-existing wakefulness is just this.

Being aware, it is cognizance,
A natural knowing that is free of thought.
This self-knowing cannot possibly form thoughts.

Without conceptualizing a "mind,"
Since it is not something to be conceived,

This original wakefulness, cognizant yet thought-free,
Is like the wisdom of the Buddha.

Therefore, it is taught, "Realize that luminous mind
Is the mind of original wakefulness,
And don't seek an enlightenment separate from it."

Nevertheless, this mind does become disturbed
By the defilement of momentary thoughts.
Like water, gold, or the sky,
It may be either pure or impure.

FROM THE SONGS OF NAROPA, GREAT INDIAN
MASTER OF THE KAGYÜ LINEAGE

Samsara

Conceptual thinking, the great ignorance,
Makes you fall into the ocean of samsara.
Once free from this conceptual thinking
You are forever beyond sorrow.[4]

DIGNAGA, INDIAN MASTER, IN HIS PRAISE
TO MANJUSHRI

Impermanence

Drops of water fall as rain,
Creating many bubbles.
These bubbles form, burst, and are no more.
Know all things to be this way.

BUDDHA SHAKYAMUNI,
King of Samadhi Sutra

Illusion

By gathering the illusory accumulations,
You become illusorily enlightened
And carry out as an illusion
The illusory welfare of beings

BUDDHA SHAKYAMUNI,
Sutra Foretelling Goodness

Stillness and Insight

Shamatha is one-pointed attention. Vipashyana is the distinct discernment of phenomena, correctly and exactly as they are.[5]

Shamatha curbs disturbing emotions, while vipashyana utterly purifies them.

BUDDHA SHAKYAMUNI,
Cloud of Jewels Sutra

In the Palm of Your Hand

When the master's words have entered your heart
You are like someone seeing a treasure in the palm of
    his hand.

SARAHA, GREAT INDIAN MASTER

To Be or Not to Be

Though the myriad worlds, in untold numbers,
Will all be destroyed in a conflagration,
Space itself does not perish.
So too is self-existing wakefulness

BUDDHA SHAKYAMUNI,
Avatamsaka Sutra

Natural Mind

Without controlling the breath or tying down your attention,
Rest in uncontrived wakefulness like a small child.

SHAVARIPA, INDIAN MAHASIDDHA

Spontaneous Song

Don't wander, don't wander, place mindfulness on guard.
Along the road of distraction, Mara lies in ambush.
Mara is this mind, clinging to like and dislike.
Free from dualistic clinging, look into the essence of this
    magic.
Realize your mind is unfabricated primordial purity.
There is no buddha elsewhere, so look into your natural
    face.
There is nothing else to search for, so rest in your natural
    state.
Nonmeditation is spontaneous perfection, so capture
    your royal seat.

DRUBWANG TSOKNYI

Padmasambhava

I will pass away to eradicate the view of permanence.
But twelve years from now, to clear away the view of
    nihilism,
I shall appear from a lotus in the immaculate Kosha Lake
As a noble son to delight the King
And turn the Dharma wheel of the unexcelled essential
    meaning.

BUDDHA SHAKYAMUNI,
Sutra of Predictions in Magadha

Natural Strength of Awareness

If the natural strength of awareness is not brought forth,
A numb and inert state of stillness will never yield any
   progress whatsoever.
So it is crucial to bring forth the steady clarity of
   awareness.
There are many meditators, but few who know how to
   meditate.

PADMASAMBHAVA

Life Is Running Out

Your mind, the primordial buddha,
Searches elsewhere due to the power of desire.
Doesn't it notice that it is wandering in samsara?

Now that you have obtained the precious human body,
You continuously get carried away by mundane actions.
Don't you notice that your life is running out?

PADMASAMBHAVA

Clinging to Emptiness

Kashyapa,[6] a belief in a self as huge as Mount Sumeru is easy to destroy, but the belief in emptiness with deep conceit is not destroyed so easily.

BUDDHA SHAKYAMUNI,
Ratnakuta Sutra

Like Cattle

To cling to a concrete reality is to be as foolish as cattle,
But clinging to emptiness is even more foolish.

Saraha

Perceiving

You are not bound by perceiving, but by clinging;
So cut your clinging, Naropa!

TILOPA

Coincidence

When the right coincidence is formed in the body,
Realization dawns in your mind.

FROM A TANTRA; OFTEN USED TO GIVE
THE PERSPECTIVE FOR YOGIC POSTURES
AND EXERCISES

Mindlessness

Your deluded mind uncontrolled by mindfulness,
Your awareness fluttering about,
Your attention like a feather blown about by the wind;
These will hardly seize the natural steadiness of the
  innate.

THE GREAT SIDDHA ORGYENPA

Direction

This unbridled stallion, your mind,
Used to gallop on errant paths.
Now steer it onto the correct track!

DÜSUM KHYENPA, THE FIRST KARMAPA

Letting Be

All your thinking is conceptual mind,
So give up the doings of this mind and rest.
And as "rest" is also just a word,
Give up holding on to words and let be.

SONGTSEN GAMPO, THE FIRST DHARMA
KING OF TIBET

Dull Stillness

You may train for a long time in dull stillness without
   clarity
And still not realize your nature.
So, actualize the gaze of sharp awareness
And meditate by repeating short sessions.

Lorepa, great meditation master

Perseverance

In order to eliminate doubt from your mind
Follow your master's advice without being lazy.
That is the guard against Mara to vanquish
    disturbing emotions.
Through it you dispel flawed beliefs and craving.
In this way strive to liberate all beings.

BUDDHA SHAKYAMUNI,
Avatamsaka Sutra

The True Training

When distracted you don't realize the natural state.
When meditating you stray into concepts or a particular
  meditation.
So train yourself in the true path:
Continuous freshness, undistracted while not meditating.

BARAWA, GREAT INDIAN MEDITATION MASTER

Noble Aspirations

Victorious ones of the three times, with your sons and
     disciples,
Divinities of the Three Roots, hosts of accomplished
     knowledge holders,
Ocean of Dharma protectors, guardians of what is
     virtuous,
Grant your blessings that this pure aspiration may be
     fulfilled.

The single cause of the benefit and welfare of countless
     beings,
The basis from which all qualities of virtuous goodness
     originate,
Is the flawless, precious teaching of the Victorious One.
May it spread and flourish throughout all times and
     directions.

May the Buddha's teachings spread completely
In accordance with all possible inclinations of sentient
     beings.
May all beings enjoy the profound and extensive
     teachings
Exactly befitting their individual intelligence and
     inclinations.

May the ultimate vehicle, the true and unexcelled meaning,
May the highest view, the wondrous Great Perfection,
May the essence of the teachings, the vajra vehicle of
    luminosity,
Spread, flourish, and remain forever.

May the ones who uphold the treasury of the qualities
    of the pure three trainings,
The doctrine holders and masters, fill all lands.
May one hundred thousand suns and moons of learning,
    reflection, and meditation rise
To let the light of the teachings illuminate all directions.

Sights and sounds are deity and mantra, and the world
    with its beings is the realm of the victorious ones.
All this is of one taste within the sphere of awareness,
The expanse of the mind of Samantabhadra, indivisible
    emptiness and cognizance.
May all beings quickly be liberated in this primordially
    pure space.

By the power of the wondrous blessings of the truth of
    the Triple Gem,
And the truth of my own pure and noble intentions,
May all these aspirations be fulfilled without obstruction,
Manifesting the auspicious circumstances for the
    Buddha's teachings to remain!

TSELE NATSOK RANGDRÖL

The Three Kayas

Within the all-pervasive space of dharmakaya,
Sambhogakaya manifests distinctly, like the light of
    the sun,
While nirmanakaya, like a rainbow, acts for the welfare
    of beings;
May the auspiciousness of the three kayas be present!

TRADITIONAL METAPHOR FOR THE THREE KAYAS,
THE "BODIES OF BUDDHAHOOD"

The Ultimate Instruction

Empty cognizance of one taste, suffused with
knowing, ⁜
Is your unmistaken nature, the uncontrived original
state. ⁜
When not altering what is, allow it to be as it is, ⁜
And the awakened state is right now spontaneously
present. ⁜

PADMASAMBHAVA,
Lamrim Yeshe Nyingpo

Ultimate Bodhichitta

Namo ❧

I and the six classes of beings, all living things, ❧
Are buddhas from the very beginning. ❧
By the nature of knowing this to be as it is, ❧
I form the resolve toward supreme enlightenment. ❧

FROM *Guhyagarbha Tantra,*
THE *Tantra of the Secret Essence*

Caring

OM KHRECHARA GHANA HUNG HRIH SVAHA

If you repeat this three times in the morning and then spit on the soles of your feet, all the insects who die that day under your feet will be reborn as gods in the realm of the Thirty-three Devas.

BUDDHA SHAKYAMUNI,
Sutra of the Celestial Palace Filled with Jewels

The Ground

The ground to be understood is the all-pervasive sugata
essence. ⁂

Unformed, luminous, and empty, it is the natural state of
awareness. ⁂

Beyond confusion and liberation, it is completely quies-
cent like space. ⁂

Although it abides without separation in samsara or
joining in nirvana, ⁂

Due to the great demons of coemergent and conceptual
ignorance, ⁂

From the solidified habitual patterns of grasping and
fixation, ⁂

And the different perceptions of worlds and
inhabitants, ⁂

The six classes of beings appeared as a dream. ⁂

Although this is so, you have never moved and will never
move ⁂

From the original condition of the essence. ⁂

Endeavor, therefore, in purifying the temporary
stains. ⁂

PADMASAMBHAVA, *Lamrim Yeshe Nyingpo*

Practitioners of Ati Yoga

It is difficult to realize the nature of Ati Yoga of the Great Perfection, so train in it! This nature is the awakened state of mind. Although your body remains human, your mind attains the state of buddhahood.

No matter how profound, vast, or all-encompassing the teachings of the Great Perfection may be, they are all included within this: Don't meditate on or fabricate even as much as an atom, and don't be distracted for even an instant.

There is a danger that people who fail to comprehend this will use this platitude: "It is all right not to meditate!" Their minds remain fettered by the distractions of samsaric business, although when someone realizes the nature of non-meditation, they should have liberated samsara and nirvana into equality. When realization occurs, you should definitely be free from samsara, so that your disturbing emotions naturally subside and become original wakefulness. What is the use of a realization that fails to reduce your disturbing emotions?

PADMASAMBHAVA

Song of Compassion

Avalokiteshvara, mighty Great Treasure of Compassion,
From my heart I invoke your blessing.
By this blessing, may compassion be born in my mind
And in the minds of all beings under the sky.

If a man has compassion, he is a buddha;
Without compassion, he is a Lord of Death.

With compassion, the root of Dharma is planted;
Without compassion, the root of Dharma is rotten.

One with compassion is kind even when angry;
One without compassion will kill even as he smiles.

For one with compassion, even enemies will turn into
    friends;
Without compassion, even friends turn into enemies.

With compassion, one has all Dharmas;
Without compassion, one has no Dharma at all.

With compassion, one is a Buddhist;
Without compassion, one is worse than a heretic.

Even if meditating on voidness, one needs compassion
    as its essence.
A Dharma practitioner must have a compassionate
    nature.

Compassion is the distinctive characteristic of
    Buddhism.
Compassion is the very essence of all Dharmas.

Great compassion is like a wish-fulfilling gem.
Great compassion will fulfill the hopes of self and
    others.

Therefore, all of you, practitioners and lay people,
Cultivate compassion and you will achieve buddhahood.

May all men and women who hear this song
With great compassion benefit all beings!

LAMA SHABKAR, FROM HIS AUTOBIOGRAPHY

Approaching Mahamudra

Look at the nature of the world,
Impermanent like a mirage or dream;
Even the mirage or dream does not exist.
Therefore, develop renunciation and abandon worldly
    activities.

Renounce servants and kin, causes of passion and
    aggression.
Meditate alone in the forest, in retreats, in solitary
    places.
Remain in the state of nonmeditation.
If you attain nonattainment, then you have attained
    Mahamudra.

TILOPA,
Mahamudra Upadesha

Nonsectarian Supplication

I supplicate all the noble doctrine holders of India, Tibet, China, Shambhala, and all other places, who follow the precious teachings of the sutras and tantras taught by the incomparable teacher who is praised like the white lotus.

I supplicate the Nyingmapas of the Secret Mantra, who uphold the sutras, mantras, and the three inner tantras in general, and especially the tradition of the Great Perfection—perfectly translated by the supreme learned and accomplished translators and panditas.

I supplicate the Kagyüpas, protectors of beings, who chiefly uphold the lineage of practice and blessing from the mahasiddhas Naropa and Maitripa, the cycles of the profound instructions and especially Mahamudra.

I supplicate the glorious Sakyapas, who illuminate the doctrine of teaching and practicing the heart extract of Lord Birwapa, the cycles of instruction in general and the path and fruit in particular.

I supplicate the Gelugpas, who mainly uphold the essence tradition of Manjushri—the key points of the path of sutra and mantra—by chiefly practicing the gradual path of glorious Atisha.

I supplicate the Jetsün Jonangpas, who chiefly uphold the meaning of the sutras of the last Dharma wheel and of the Kalachakra, who have realized the truth of the sugata essence and possess the vajra yoga.

Impartially I supplicate all the doctrine holders, each and every one, who exist in these snowy ranges, of the Glorious Shangpa, Chöyul, Shije, Nyendrub, and the other cycles of profound instructions.[7]

By the blessings of making these supplications, may sectarianism be calmed and may impartial devotion blaze forth. May all the doctrine holders be in harmony and may all countries be peaceful. May the auspicious circumstance in which the teachings may flourish for a long time be present.

DZONGSAR KHYENTSE CHÖKYI LODRÖ

Emptiness and Compassion

From the wish-fulfilling tree of emptiness
Appear the fruits of nonconceptual compassion.
This is the root of all the awakened ones.
From this they emerge, there is no doubt.

FROM THE *Scripture in Five Hundred Thousand Verses,*
THE MEDIUM-LENGTH VERSION
OF THE *Hevajra Tantra*

Source of All Speech

A is the supreme syllable,
The sacred syllable of all meaning.
Arising from within, it is without arising.
Beyond verbal expression,
It is the supreme cause of all expressions.

FROM THE *Tantra of the Magical Net of Manjushri*

Fourteen Meaningless Things

Like returning empty-handed from an island of precious
      gems, it is meaningless to ignore the sacred Dharma
      after having obtained a human body.

Like a moth diving into a flame, it is meaningless to return
      to family life after having entered the gateway to the
      Dharma.

Like dying of thirst at the shore of the ocean, it is mean-
      ingless to live near a noble Dharma master while hav-
      ing no trust.

Like leaning an axe against a tree trunk, it is meaningless to
      have a spiritual practice that is not used to remedy the
      four roots and ego-clinging.

Like a sick person holding a bag of medicines, it is mean-
      ingless to have heard oral instructions that don't rem-
      edy disturbing emotions.

Like a parrot reciting verses, it is meaningless to have a
      tongue that expertly recites Dharma words that are
      not taken to heart.

Like trying to wash a sheepskin coat in plain water,[8] it is
      meaningless to be generous with wealth acquired
      through thievery, robbery, or deception.

Like handing a mother her child's flesh, it is meaningless to
      make offerings to the Three Jewels by hurting other
      sentient beings.

Like a cat lying in wait for a mouse, it is meaningless to be
stubbornly involved in selfish aims for this life.
Like trading a wish-fulfilling jewel for a pile of ordinary
gems, a load of leftover beer-mash, or a single bag
of flour, it is meaningless to perform ostentatious
virtuous actions out of a desire for mundane praise
and fame, honor and gain.
Like a doctor stricken by an incurable disease, it is meaningless to have studied a lot and yet remain a shallow
person.
Like a rich man without the key to his treasury, it is meaningless to be learned in the oral instructions but not
apply them in practice.
Like the blind leading the blind, it is meaningless to teach
others the significance of a spiritual practice you
haven't realized yourself.
Like believing brass to be gold, it is meaningless to regard
an experience produced through a technique to be the
supreme, while neglecting the natural state.
These were the fourteen things that are meaningless.

GAMPOPA

Space of Mind

Just as the sky is all-pervading
And has a nonconceptual nature,
The immaculate space of the mind's nature
Is similarly all-pervading.

MAITREYA, *Uttaratantra,*
RECORDED BY THE INDIAN MASTER ASANGA

Giving Protection from Fear

Giving protection from fear means actually doing whatever you can to help others in difficulty. It includes, for instance, providing a refuge for those without any place of safety, giving protection to those without any protector, and being with those who have no other companion. In particular, it refers to such actions as forbidding hunting and fishing wherever you have the power to do so, buying back sheep on the way to slaughter, and saving the lives of dying fish, worms, flies, and other creatures. For the Buddha taught that, of all relative good actions, saving lives is the most beneficial.

PATRUL RINPOCHE

Our Buddha Nature

The buddha nature present in sentient beings is like the sky.
As the sky has no past, present, or future, neither inside nor
outside, and is not composed of form, sound, smell, taste, or
texture, so also is the buddha nature.

BUDDHA SHAKYAMUNI,
Mahaparinirvana Sutra

The Sugata Essence

Pure, crystal-clear, and luminous,
Undisturbed and uncompounded;
This, the sugata essence,
Is the nature that is primordially present.

BUDDHA SHAKYAMUNI,
King of Samadhi Sutra

Theory, Experience, and Realization

Theories are like a patch; they wear and fall off.
Experiences are like mist; they fade and vanish.
Realization is like space—unchanging.

EARLY MASTERS OF THE PRACTICE LINEAGE

Compassion

If you possess one quality, it would be as if you had all enlightened qualities in the very palm of your hand. Which
quality? Great compassion.

BUDDHA SHAKYAMUNI,
Sutra That Expresses Avalokiteshvara's Realization

Heart Advice

Although your realization is equal to that of the buddhas, make offerings to the Three Jewels. Although you have gained mastery over your mind, direct your innermost aims toward the Dharma. Although the nature of the Great Perfection is supreme, don't disparage other teachings.

Although you have realized that buddhas and sentient beings are equal, embrace all beings with compassion. Although the paths and bhumis are beyond training and traversing, don't forsake purifying your obscurations through Dharma activities. Although the accumulations are beyond gathering, don't sever the roots of conditioned virtue.

Although your mind lies beyond birth and death, this illusory body does die, so practice while remembering death. Although you experience your innate nature free from thought, maintain the attitude of bodhichitta. Although you have attained the fruition of dharmakaya, keep company with your yidam deity.

Although dharmakaya is not some other place, seek the true meaning. Although buddhahood is nowhere else, dedicate any virtue you create toward unexcelled enlightenment. Although everything experienced is original wakefulness, don't let your mind stray into samsara.

Although your mind essence is the awakened one, always worship the deity and your master. Although you have real-

ized the nature of the Great Perfection, don't abandon your
yidam deity. Those who, instead of doing this, speak fool-
ishly with boastful words only damage the Three Jewels and
will not find even an instant of happiness.

PADMASAMBHAVA

The Roots of Ego

You may repeatedly burn down the jungle of disturbing emotions with the wildfire of meditative concentration, but it grows back the moment the rain comes down, because you have not abandoned the firm roots of ego-belief.

ARYADEVA, EARLY INDIAN MASTER

The Gradual Path

Like ascending the steps of a staircase,
You should also train step-by-step
And endeavor in my profound teachings;
Without jumping any steps, proceed gradually to the end.

Just as a small child
Gradually develops its body and strength,
So does one's Dharma practice,
From the first steps of entering
Up until the complete perfection.

BUDDHA SHAKYAMUNI,
Nirvana Sutra

The Most Precious Attitude

There is not a single one among all sentient beings, who pervade to the farthest reaches of the sky, who has not been our own mother and father. Not just once or a few times, but since beginningless samsara until now, the times they have been so are beyond count. Apart from establishing them in the supreme state of enlightenment, we cannot just forsake them, and no other means whatsoever will repay their kindness.

Consequently, the time has come for us to be the guiding defender for all these countless sentient beings, our own parents. In order to do so, we ourselves must attain the sublime nirvana that dwells in neither the extreme of nirvanic peace nor samsaric existence. The primary cause and method for this attainment is no other than this precious attitude of bodhichitta.

TSELE NATSOK RANGDRÖL

Phenomena

All phenomena are circumstantial
And depend completely on your attitude.

From the *Lamp of the Three Methods*

Bodhichitta

All the phenomena of samsara and nirvana ultimately do not transcend being natural emptiness free from all constructed limitations. Nevertheless, the manifold ways of samsara and nirvana, self and others, pleasure and pain, and so forth manifest out of the unobstructed medium of superficial experience. No matter how these are experienced, in actuality they don't possess even as much as an atom of true existence! While nonexistent, they are experienced, and while experienced, they do not possess any existence—this is a characteristic of all things. Though this is so, sentient beings do not realize it, and therefore they attach solid reality to the habitual tendencies of erring in regard to these nonexistent experiences. And so they constantly undergo the endless suffering of samsara. Since these beings are all exclusively my own kind parents, I must establish them in well-being! Since I personally don't possess the ability to do so, I will now form the resolve, which I previously did not have, to endeavor to quickly attain the state of enlightenment, now that the auspicious causes and conditions for doing so are present! In this way, I will attain buddhahood for the welfare of sentient beings!

TSELE NATSOK RANGDRÖL

This Fleeting Life

Like the mountain river flowing into the ocean,
Like the sun or moon approaching the western
    mountain,
Like day and night, hours and minutes pass quickly by,
As does the life of every person.

FROM THE *Vinaya Scripture*

Good and Evil

Attachment, anger, and delusion
And the actions created by them are unvirtuous.
From nonvirtue comes suffering,
As do all evil states.

Nonattachment, nonanger, and nondelusion
And the actions created by them are virtuous.
From virtue come the happy states
And happiness in all rebirths.

NAGARJUNA,
Jewel Garland

Equality

Kashyapa, you transcend suffering when you realize all things to be the nature of equality. This equality is but one; it is neither two nor three.

Buddha Shakyamuni,
Sutra Requested by Kashyapa

Saving Lives

By your saving the lives of birds, fish, and deer,
Or thieves, snakes, and others to be killed,
Your life will presently be extended,
Even though it would otherwise be short.

In this way, all the sutras and tantras teach that the supreme among all types of longevity practices is to save the lives of sentient beings who are certain to be killed. This can also be established through intelligent reasoning. For this reason and because freeing lives brings immeasurable benefits, all sensible people should bolster their efforts to free lives.

JAMYANG KHYENTSE WANGPO

Nagarjuna's Realization

It was then that Nagarjuna, a monk learned in the five topics of knowledge, who had understood the meaning of the Tripitaka, and who knew numerous resultant teachings on Secret Mantra, went in search of the meaning of the effortless Great Perfection. After meeting the nun Dagnyima, he requested the meaning of realization from her; she then bestowed it in full and condensed the meaning for him in song:

> While reflecting, you may understand emptiness,
> > but it is still confusion.
> While clinging, you may cling to the view, but it is
> > still a fetter.
> While thinking, you may understand dharmakaya,
> > but it is still a thought.
> While meditating, you may cultivate nonthought,
> > but it is still conceptual.

Thus she sang.

Nagarjuna understood the basic intent and then expressed his realization:

> I am Nagarjuna,
> Who is at ease since nonarising dharmakaya is
> > beyond the aggregates.

I am at ease since my unvoiced, unceasing speech is
     beyond conceptual attributes,
And I am at ease since my thought-free mind of
     wisdom is beyond birth and death.
I have realized that awakened mind is great bliss.

DAGNYIMA AND NAGARJUNA, EARLY MASTERS
     IN THE TRANSMISSION OF THE DZOGCHEN
     TEACHINGS, FROM *Wellsprings of Perfection*

Precious Human Body

To obtain a human body is extremely difficult, so it is foolish to ignore the Dharma upon having found it. Only the Dharma can help you; everything else is worldly beguilement.

PADMASAMBHAVA

The Four Immeasurables

A bodhisattva mahasattva should cultivate great love, great compassion, great joy and great impartiality.

BUDDHA SHAKYAMUNI,
Medium-Length Prajnaparamita

Love and the other three, when not embraced by generating bodhichitta, are merely causes for happiness within samsaric existence and are therefore called the four Brahma abodes. When embraced by the bodhichitta resolve, these four are causes for nirvana and therefore called the four immeasurables.

BUDDHA SHAKYAMUNI,
Supreme Essence Sutra

Taking Care of Business

Take advice from others;
Make the decisions yourself.

TIBETAN SAYING, QUOTED BY
CHÖKYI NYIMA RINPOCHE

The Merit of Bodhichitta

Were the merit of bodhichitta
To have a physical form,
It would fill the entire expanse of space
And be greater even than that.

BUDDHA SHAKYAMUNI

The Six Paramitas

Subahu, in order to awaken to true and complete enlightenment, a bodhisattva mahasattva should always and continually train in the six paramitas.

BUDDHA SHAKYAMUNI

Song to Mandarava

Listen here a while, Mandarava flower!
Pay heed without distraction, perfect princess!

You have wandered in samsara, in the miseries of
    existence,
Like an ocean without escape, for so long.
Now is the time to achieve the lasting aim.
You must practice the divine Dharma, young princess!

There's no end to the tasks and deeds of this world,
And you have pointlessly occupied yourself for so long.
Now is the time to think in different ways.
You must reach liberation, young princess!

By the power of attachment, you have yearned for
    relatives
And nurtured thankless companions for so long.
Now is the time to train in lucid emptiness.
You must look into your mind, young princess!

By the power of anger, you have raged against enemies,
And brought ruin to yourself and others for so long.
Now is the time to tame your own emotions.
You must soften your selfishness, young princess!

By the power of delusion, you have drifted in samsara's
    common states
And slept like a shameless corpse for so long.
Now is the time to persevere in the undistracted practice.
You must bring forth your bright best, young princess!

By the power of conceit, you have taken the high seat of
    influence,
Giving lofty advice to others for so long.
Now is the time to be a counsel to yourself.
You must repel your own faults, young princess!

By the power of jealousy, you have disparaged others
And engaged in rivalry for so long.
Now is the time to follow in the footsteps of the
    conquerors.
You must train in pure perception, young princess!

While creating evil karma, you have floundered in the
    ocean of samsara,
Taking inferior rebirths for so long.
Now is the time to train in the deity's form of empty
    presence.
Cultivate the development stage, young princess!

Deluded idle gossip promotes only more conditioned
    states,
And you have given yourself to endless chatter for
    so long.

Now is the time to chant the essence mantra of empty
    sound.
Keep this in your mind, young princess!

Through so many thoughts, myriad emotions arise,
And you have submitted yourself to deluded thinking
    for so long.
Now is the time to capture the kingdom of empty bliss.
Train in the nonarising nature, young princess!

The profound vehicle is like taking a precious shortcut.
While you have the chance to enter this path,
Now is the time to train in all-pervasive pure perception.
Generate devotion, young princess!

PADMASAMBHAVA,
Golden Garland Chronicles, HIS BIOGRAPHY

The Four Principles of a Spiritual Practitioner

Don't retaliate with anger when attacked with rage.
Do not retaliate with abuse when reviled.
Do not retaliate with criticism when blamed in public.
Don't retaliate with blows when threatened with physical
   violence.

BUDDHA SHAKYAMUNI

The Four Immeasurables

May all beings have happiness and the cause of happiness.
May they be free of suffering and the cause of suffering.
May they not be apart from the sublime happiness that
is free of suffering.
May they remain in the great equanimity free from bias
and partiality.

TRADITIONAL CHANT, REPEATED SIX TIMES A DAY

Noble Wishes in Daily Life

When putting on clothes, make the wish: May we don the
garment of conscience and propriety!

When tying your belt, make the wish: May we fasten the belt
of the vows and precepts!

When opening a door, make the wish: May we open the
door of the profound innate nature!

When closing it, make the wish: May we close the door to
the lower realms!

When walking, make the wish: May we move forward on the
path of enlightenment!

When riding, make the wish: May we ride the horse of diligence!

When crossing water, make the wish: May we cross the ocean
of samsara!

When walking upward or ascending a staircase, make the
wish: May we ascend on the path of liberation!

When arriving at the desired destination, make the wish:
May we arrive at the city of nirvana!

When meeting a master or noble beings, make the wish: May
we meet with a true master and be accepted by him!

When visiting a shrine for the Three Jewels, make the wish:
May we take rebirth in a pure buddhafield!

When on a journey or going to sleep, make the wish: May we
rest on the path of the Dharma!

BUDDHA SHAKYAMUNI, *Avatamsaka Sutra*, FROM THE
CHAPTER ON TOTALLY PURE CONDUCT

Mind Essence

Where the past has ceased and the future has not yet
    arisen, ᛯ
In the unimpeded state of present wakefulness, ᛯ
Rest in the manner of mind looking into mind. ᛯ
No matter what thoughts may arise at this time, ᛯ
They are all the display of the single mind essence. ᛯ
As the nature of space is unchanging, ᛯ
You will realize the all-pervasive mind essence to be
    changeless. ᛯ
This is the Great Perfection, the ultimate of all
    vehicles, ᛯ
The unexcelled meaning of the self-existing Mind
    Section. ᛯ [9]

Padmasambhava

Exchanging Oneself with Others

One who desires to quickly protect
Himself as well as all others
Should practice the secret excellence
Of exchanging himself with others.

Whatever happiness exists in the world,
All results from wishing others to be happy.
Whatever suffering exists in the world,
All results from desiring happiness for oneself.

Without fully exchanging
Your happiness for the suffering of others,
You will not accomplish buddhahood
And will find no happiness in samsara.

SHANTIDEVA

The Unity of Shamatha and Vipashyana

Shamatha is generally held to mean abiding in the state of bliss, clarity, and nonthought after conceptual thinking has naturally subsided. Vipashyana means to see nakedly and vividly the essence of mind that is self-cognizant, objectless, and free from exaggeration and denigration. Put another way, shamatha is said to be the absence of thought activity, and vipashyana is recognizing the essence of thought. Numerous other such statements exist, but, in actuality, whatever manifests or is experienced does not transcend the inseparability of shamatha and vipashyana. Both stillness and thinking are nothing but the display of the mind alone; to recognize your essence at the time of either stillness or thinking is itself the nature of vipashyana.

Shamatha is not to become involved in solidified clinging to any of the external appearances of the six collections, while vipashyana is the unobstructed manifestation of perception. Thus within perception the unity of shamatha and vipashyana is complete.

Vividly recognizing the essence of a thought as it suddenly occurs is shamatha. Directly liberating it within natural mind, free from concepts, is vipashyana. Thus within conceptual thinking shamatha and vipashyana are also a unity.

Furthermore, looking into the essence without solidly

following after a disturbing emotion even when it arises intensely is shamatha. The empty and cognizant nakedness within which the observing awareness and the observed disturbing emotion have no separate existence is vipashyana. Thus the unity of shamatha and vipashyana is complete within disturbing emotions as well.

Tsele Natsok Rangdröl

Victory and Defeat

Give gain and victory to others.
Take loss and defeat upon yourself.

ATISHA

Samsaric Pursuit

It only ends when you stop.

VIMALAMITRA

The True View

Manjushri, whoever sees all things as being without inequality, without duality, and without it being possible to separate into duality, that person is the one who has the true view.

BUDDHA SHAKYAMUNI,
Sutra of Showing the Way to Enlightenment

Song of Karma Chagmey

Emaho!

The sutras, tantras, and philosophical scriptures are
    extensive and great in number.

However, life is short and intelligence limited, so it is
    hard to cover them completely.

You may know a lot, but if you don't put it into practice,

It's like dying of thirst on the shore of a great lake.

Likewise, it sometimes happens that a common corpse is
    found in the bed of a great scholar.

The scriptures of the sutras and tantras and the words of
    the learned and accomplished ones of India and Tibet,

All have great blessings but are difficult for ordinary
    people to grasp.

Though they are indispensable for teaching in a
    monastic college,

For one-pointed practice they are of little use.

This "pointing-out instruction for an old lady" is more
    beneficial for your mind than all the others.

All the innumerable and profound teachings, such as
    Mahamudra and Dzogchen,

Which are decisive and unmistaken in each root text,

Are indispensable when teaching disciples who will hold
    the Dharma lineages.
But for personal practice, for the sake of the future,
It is more profound to condense them all into one.

To grasp precisely and unmistakenly the various
    traditions of the Dharma
Is necessary for upholding the doctrinal teachings.
But if you are concerned with your future welfare,
It is more profound to train in being nonsectarian, seeing
    all of them as pure.

It is necessary to focus your mind on one single and
    sufficient master
If you are to be his chief disciple.
But if you wish to have the virtues of experience and
    realization dawn within you,
It is more profound to combine all the teachers you have
    met into one
And to visualize him as the Buddha resting on your
    crown and to supplicate him.

The different recitations for various development stage
    practices
Of numerous yidam deities in the sections of tantra
Are indispensable if you are to give empowerments as a
    great master.
But as a means for purifying your own obscurations and
    attaining accomplishment,

It is more profound to practice one deity and mantra
that includes them all.

The innumerable practices of the completion stage, with
and without reference point,
Are indispensable for expounding the countless meditation manuals.
But as a means for the virtues of experience and realization to dawn within you,
It is more profound to sustain the essence, which is the
embodiment of them all.

There are many ways of demonstrating the view,
Such as cutting through fabrications from outside and
from within.
But, just as smoke vanishes when the flames in a fireplace
are extinguished,
It is more profound to cut through the root
of mind.

Although there are numerous meditation techniques,
both with and without concepts,
It is more profound to practice the unity of luminosity
and emptiness,
The development stage completed by mere recollection.

Although there are numerous kinds of behavior, high
and low, coarse and precise,
It is more profound to exert yourself as much as you can

in practicing virtue and abandoning evil deeds.
Although numerous details have been taught about attainment, the time of reaching fruition,
It is more profound to possess the definite certainty
of attainmen
After having unmistakenly practiced the view, meditation, and action.

Although bodhisattvas who have accomplished the levels
Are not obscured even by serious wrongdoing or mis-
deeds done for the sake of the teachings,
Since someone like us has to fear the lower realms,
It is more profound to shun, without involvement,
wrongdoing and severe faults.

Moreover, without self-interest and for the general benefit of beings,
It is profound to seal your practices, such as offering and
giving, copying teachings, and reciting texts,
With a dedication free from conceptualizing the three
spheres.

KARMA CHAGMEY,
The Union of Mahamudra and Dzogchen

Dependent Origination and Emptiness

There exist no phenomena that do not originate in
dependency.
Therefore there exist no phenomena that are not
emptiness.

NAGARJUNA

From Drops of Water

If you want to genuinely practice the Dharma, do what is virtuous, even the most minute deed. Renounce what is evil, even the tiniest deed. The largest ocean is made from drops of water; even Mount Sumeru and the four continents are made of tiny atoms.

It doesn't matter whether your act of giving is as small as a single sesame seed; if you give with compassion and bodhichitta, you achieve hundredfold merit. If you give without the bodhichitta resolve, your merit will not increase even if you give away horses and cattle.

PADMASAMBHAVA

Compounded Things

Like a star, an aberration, or a flame,
Like a magical illusion, a dewdrop, or a water bubble,
Like a dream, lightning, or a cloud,
Know all things to be this way.

BUDDHA SHAKYAMUNI,
King of Samadhi Sutra

Shri Singha's Instruction

Padmasambhava further asked: "Great master, how is the nature of the mind of buddhas and sentient beings?"

Shri Singha replied: "The nature of the mind of buddhas and sentient beings does not consist of any entity whatsoever. Yet, while it is not a real entity, I have not found it to be in one absolute way. When one fails to find a reference point in the mind, something to identify, conceptions are liberated in themselves; there is no demon who can harm it. That is called 'cutting through outer misconceptions.'

"This is the way to cut through inner misconceptions: This self-existing wakefulness of knowing cannot be found to have arisen from a particular cause, to have been produced from certain conditions, or to possess such and such an identity. Even I, Shri Singha, have not discovered any mind that could be described as being such and such. So, Padmasambhava, I too have no mind to show you as being in any one absolute way."

Having spoken in this way, he dissolved into indestructible space.

SHRI SINGHA

Transcendent Knowledge

This cultivation of transcendent knowledge is to cultivate no concept whatsoever.

BUDDHA SHAKYAMUNI,
Sutra of Prajnaparamita in Eight Thousand Verses

The Nature of Things

Sentient beings exclaim, "I see the sky!"
But one must examine the meaning of exactly how the
sky is seen;
This is how the tathagata describes the way we see
phenomena.

FROM THE *Compendium of Prajnaparamita*

Buddhas in Waiting

All beings are indeed buddhas,
But they are covered by temporary obscurations.
When these are removed, they are really buddhas.

FROM THE *Hevajra Tantra*

Spiritual Teachers

Ananda, the Awakened Ones do not appear to all sentient beings, but they teach the Dharma and plant the seeds of liberation by appearing as spiritual teachers. Therefore, regard a spiritual teacher as superior to all tathagatas.

BUDDHA SHAKYAMUNI,
Sutra of Immaculate Space

All Things Pass

The three worlds are impermanent like the clouds
    of autumn.
The births and deaths of beings are like watching a
    dance.
The life span of people is like a flash of lightning
    in the sky,
And like a waterfall, it is quickly gone.

BUDDHA SHAKYAMUNI,
Lalitavistara Sutra

Preparing for Death

Spend all your food supplies and wealth on virtuous deeds. Some people say, "One needs wealth at the time of death." But when you are struck by a fatal sickness, you cannot apportion your pain out for money, no matter how many helpers you have, and your pain is no greater if you have none.

At that time it makes no difference whether you have helpers, servants, attendants, and wealth. All are causes for attachment. Attachment binds you, even attachment to your deity and to the Dharma. The rich person's attachment to his thousand ounces of gold and the poor man's attachment to his needle and thread are equally binding. Give up the attachment that blocks the door to liberation.

When you die, it is the same whether your body is cremated on a pyre of sandalwood or consumed by birds and dogs in an unpeopled place. You go on, accompanied by whatever good or evil deeds you committed while alive. Your bad name or good reputation, your stock of food and wealth, and all your helpers and servants are left behind.

On the day you die, you will need a sublime master, so seek one out beforehand. Without a master you cannot possibly awaken to enlightenment, so follow a qualified master and carry out whatever he suggests.

Padmasambhava

Spontaneous Song

The mighty Vajradhara of the definitive meaning,
The ultimate realization of Samantabhadra,
Is directly pointed out as my natural face by the guru.
I remember my guide, who is like a second Garab
    Dorje.[10]

The heart of the eighty-four thousand teachings of the
    victorious ones
Is the excellent path of the Great Perfection.
To naturally liberate without rejecting the deluded
    thoughts of fixation—
That is the greatness of the oral instruction.

There is no choosing between the phenomena of sam-
    sara and nirvana.
When reassuming the natural abode in our innate
    essence,
The king of fruition is discovered within ourselves;
What a joy to accomplish the aims of a happy mind!

While realizing that self-awareness is the guru,
I supplicate him with the free-flowing natural state.
Cutting through the sidetracks of conceptual mind,
Let us arrive at the state of nonmeditation.

JIGDREL YESHE DORJE, DUDJOM RINPOCHE

Mortality

On this earth, or even in the higher realms,
Have you ever seen or heard of
Someone who once born would not die,
Or do you ever have any doubt about it?

NAGARJUNA,
Letter for Dispelling Sorrow

Song of Openness

Samsara and nirvana are indivisible within the continuity
of awareness,
Basically unborn, the state of exhausted phenomena
beyond concepts.
This innate mode of awareness, free from the entities of
perceiver and perceived,
In a nakedness that is unending and all-pervasive, is
utterly open!

All appearances are baseless, empty forms,
Nonexistent and yet vividly present, like a magical
illusion or the moon in water.
Visible and yet unreal, they never existed in the ground,
But in a nakedness that is empty and without entity, they
are utterly open!

Whatever appears is an unconfined continuity of empty
natural cognizance.
Thoughts and memories vanish, empty and traceless like
the sky.
Cognition and mental states are baseless, rootless, and
intangible.
Empty and devoid of an entity to grasp, they are utterly
open!

LONGCHEN RABJAM,
Space without Center or Edge

Tara

The venerable Arya Tara is the wisdom form of all the buddhas and bodhisattvas of the ten directions. In the ultimate sense, she has, since primordial time, attained the state of original wakefulness that is the very essence of the female buddha Prajnaparamita. However, to portray her background in a way that ordinary disciples can comprehend, here is her story.

Long ago, in a past eon, in the world Myriad Lights, there was a buddha known as Drum Thunder. It was in the presence of this buddha that she was the princess Wisdom Moon and first formed the resolve to attain supreme enlightenment, and here she took the oath to work for the welfare of all beings in the form of a woman until the whole of samsara is emptied. In accordance with her vow, she practiced day and night and became able to liberate, every day, one hundred billion sentient beings from their mundane frame of mind and make them attain "the acceptance of the nonarising of all things." Through this she was given the name Arya Tara, the Sublime Savior, the mere recalling of whose name invokes the blessings to dispel both samsara's suffering and the shortcomings of the passive state of nirvana.

After that she took the vow in front of Buddha Amoghasiddhi to protect the beings of the ten directions from fear and all kinds of harm. On another occasion, she acted as an emanation of Avalokiteshvara's wisdom in order to assist him in working for the liberation of all beings. In this way, her life examples surpass the reach of ordinary thought.

Particularly in this world, during the Golden Age the compassionate Avalokiteshvara taught one hundred million Vajrayana tantras of Tara on Mount Potala in India and has continued up through this Age of Strife to teach medium and concise versions that accord with people's capacity. These practices pacify the eight and sixteen types of fear and cause a wish-fulfilling attainment of all needs and aims. Ultimately, one can realize the wisdom body of Mahamudra. There are innumerable wonderful stories of past practitioners to support this.

In short, since Arya Tara is the activity of all buddhas embodied in a single form, her blessings are swifter than those of any other deity. Most of the learned and accomplished masters of India and Tibet kept her as their main practice and attained siddhi. That is why we today have such a boundless supply of practices and instructions of Arya Tara.

KHAKYAB DORJE, THE FIFTEENTH KARMAPA

Supplication to Tara

Sublime and noble Lady, with your retinue,
Please regard us with compassion, free of thought.
Bless me so the objectives of my prayer
May be unobstructedly fulfilled.

May the Buddha's teachings spread and flourish!
May its holders live in harmony and good health!
May obstacles that threaten them subside!
May their activities of teaching and practice prosper!

May sickness and famine, fighting and strife all recede!
May spiritual richness increase even further!
May the spiritual rulers' kingdoms expand!
May every country near and far have harmony!

Protect us from the sixteen threats and from untimely
    death,
From menacing dreams and from sinister omens,
From the miseries of samsara's lower realms;
From every peril, now and always!

Increase our life, merit, capacity, experience, and
    realization!
May harmful notions not intrude!

May the twofold awakened mind arise, free of effort!
May our aims be fulfilled in accordance with the
Dharma!

From now until supreme enlightenment,
As a mother protects her only child,
Guard us always with your kindness!
Let us be indivisible from you!

TRADITIONAL DAILY CHANT

All Composite Things Will Perish

At the invitation of the king, Padmasambhava joined him, his queens, and his offspring at Chimphu and participated in one hundred eight feast offerings. At this time Princess Pema Sal, the daughter of the late queen Lady Jangchub Men of Dro, who was eight years of age, passed away. When the king saw her dead body, he fell to the ground and wept. Tsogyal took a white silken cloth and sprinkled him with saffron water. When he had regained his senses, Padmasambhava spoke:

Listen, your majesty.
In general, all mundane pursuits are like dreams.
The mark of composite things is that they are like
    a magical illusion.
Your kingdom is like last night's dream.
Your wealth and your subjects are like dewdrops on
    a blade of grass.
This fleeting life is like foam on water.
All composite things will perish.
Meeting ends in separation.
All composite things are like this.
There is not a single thing that is stable and lasts.
Do not cling to the impermanent as being
    permanent.
Train in the nonarising nature of dharmakaya.

Thus he spoke. Again the master sang to the king:

Emaho,
Your majesty, great king, listen once more!
Since samsaric things have no essence,
To continue endlessly spinning about brings fur-
    ther and further suffering,
So capture the royal stronghold of dharmakaya.

As your essential homeland, keep the nonarising
    dharmadhatu.
As your essential dwelling, adhere to forest retreats
    and remote places.
As your essential retreat, look into the empty and
    luminous nature of things.
As your essential house, remain in your original
    mind nature.

As your essential bounty, keep attentive and
    mindful.
As your essential treasury, form the resolve of the
    twofold awakened mind.
As your essential wealth, keep to the two accumulations.
As your essential farming, endeavor in the ten
    spiritual practices.

As your essential fatherhood, embrace all beings
    with compassion.
As your essential motherhood, sustain the natural
    state of emptiness.

As your essential offspring, practice development and completion indivisibly.

As your essential spouse, train in bliss, clarity, and nonthought.

As your essential companion, read the scriptures of the sugatas.

As your essential farmland, cultivate unshakable faith.

As your essential food, eat the ambrosia of nonarising dharmata.

As your essential beverage, drink the nectar of oral instructions.

As your essential clothing, wear the garment of modesty and decorum.

As your essential retinue, keep dakinis and protectors of the Dharma.

As your essential enjoyment, engage in spiritual practices.

As your essential spectacle, look into your own mind.

As your essential diversion, engage in elaborate spiritual pursuits.

As your essential entertainment, train in emanating and absorbing the development stage.

As your essential close friend, keep to the empowerments and samayas.

As your essential prejudice, use the five poisons for training.

As your essential ornament, study and reflect free
from partiality.

As your essential activity, have the profound
scriptures copied.

As your essential caller, be generous without
bounds.

As your essential pursuit, direct your innermost
aim to the Dharma.

As your essential court chaplain, venerate the Three
Jewels.

As your essential objects of respect, treat your
parents with reverence.

As your essential object of honor, respect your
vajra master.

As your essential samaya, keep your mind free from
hypocrisy.

As your essential precept, give up all evil.

As your essential temple, keep the three precepts
purely.

As your essential mandala, look into the
unchanging luminosity.

As your essential instruction, tame your own mind.

As your essential view, look into the changeless,
empty cognizance.

As your essential meditation, let your mind nature
be as it is.

As your essential conduct, let the delusion of
dualistic fixation collapse.

As your essential fruition, don't seek the result that
　　is spontaneously present.

If you practice like this you will be happy in this
　　life, joyful in the next,
And soon attain complete enlightenment.

Having heard this, the king was delighted and made many
prostrations and circumambulations.

PADMASAMBHAVA

The Nature of Mind

NAMO GURU MANJUSHRIYE

This original mind, free and unformed,
Is not revealed through words but individually known
And understood without effort when receiving your
    guru's blessings.
Once you see this nature, know how to keep it without
    contrivance!

Do not keep it with the thought "I must keep natural
    mind!"
Also do not think, "I shouldn't keep hold of it!"
Leave it freely to itself, and it is clarified by itself.
This yoga of self-remaining naturalness is the supreme
    meditation!

Once you grow used to that, this original state of non-
    doing
Is neither helped nor harmed by the various thoughts,
Like clouds floating by in the vastness of the sky.
That is the time of ease for the carefree yogi—alala!

This essential advice is given to the children of my heart.

JAMGÖN MIPHAM RINPOCHE

Inspiration to Practice

Once impermanence has been taken to heart,
First, it causes you to enter Dharma practice.
Second, it becomes a spur to perseverance.
Finally, it makes you attain the luminous dharmakaya.

PHADAMPA SANGYE

View and Conduct

Although the view should be higher than the sky,
The cause and effect of actions should be finer than
flour.

PADMASAMBHAVA

Past Mothers

Although you roll the entire earth into pills the size of
    juniper fruits,
They will not equal the number of your past mothers.

NAGARJUNA

Ultimate Agreement

The Middle Way, the unity of the two truths beyond
    limitations;
Mahamudra, the basic wakefulness of the uncontrived
    natural state;
And the Great Perfection, the original Samantabhadra of
    primordial purity—
Are all in agreement on a single identical meaning.

TSELE NATSOK RANGDRÖL

Supplication

Kindest guru of incomparable and matchless
   benevolence,
Remain constantly seated as my crown ornament.
Let the illuminating daylight of the profound blessings
   of the mind transmission
Quickly enter my heart, conferring the empowerment of
   wisdom!

May my mind be softened by trust and compassion,
   renunciation and bodhichitta,
By the path of the four empowerments, perfecting
   development and completion,
And by being established in the ultimate royal palace of
   the primordial dharmakaya.
Bestow your blessings that my mind may be mingled
   with yours!

DILGO KHYENTSE RINPOCHE

Master and Disciple

Not to examine the master is like drinking poison.
Not to examine the disciple is like jumping into an
  abyss.

PADMASAMBHAVA

The Noble Resolve

Wherever space pervades it is filled with sentient beings. Wherever sentient beings pervade they are filled with evil karma and suffering. All these sentient beings who are pervaded by evil karma and suffering, without exception, have bestowed upon me the kindness of repeatedly being my fathers and mothers. Each time they were my parents they benefited me immeasurably, just like my present father and mother. Protecting me from numerous dangers, they cared for me painstakingly, as if it were their own life. How pitiful are all these beings, my kind mothers, who want happiness but create suffering and are therefore like madmen, their intentions contradicting their own actions!

But just pitying them won't help. I must lead them away from the miseries of samsara and quickly establish them in unexcelled complete enlightenment! Right now I don't have the power to do that, so within this very lifetime I will attain the state of buddhahood, which is able to liberate all beings! And therefore I will practice the profound yoga.

JAMGÖN MIPHAM RINPOCHE

Devotion and Blessings

If the sun of devotion does not shine
On the snow mountain of the guru's four kayas,[11]
The rivers of blessings will not flow.
Therefore, be diligent in devotion.

DRIGUNG KYOBPA SUMGÖN

Fear and Deathless Realization

Dying being my only fear,
I trained my mind in the innate state beyond death
And recognized the essential meaning,
The basic nature of self-liberated samsara.

Unsupported and naked inner awareness,
Discursiveness cleared, the confidence of the view—
I have resolved this to be luminous emptiness.
Now birth and death no longer intimidate me.

MILAREPA

Dedication of Merit

Just as a drop of water falling into the great ocean
Is never depleted before the ocean dries up,
Likewise, the virtue you fully dedicate to enlightenment
Is never depleted before enlightenment is attained.

BUDDHA SHAKYAMUNI,
Sutra Requested by Wisdom Ocean

Dedication

By this virtue may all beings perfect the accumulations of
merit and wisdom
And may they attain the sacred two kayas resulting from
that merit and wisdom.

NAGARJUNA

Transcendent Knowledge

Transcendent knowledge is beyond thought, word, or
   description.
It neither arises nor ceases, like the identity of space.
It is the domain of individual, self-knowing wakefulness.
I salute this mother of the buddhas of the three times.

SHANTARAKSHITA, IN PRAISE OF
                PRAJNAPARAMITA

The Apology within the Expanse of the View

When not realizing the nature of nonarising, ༔
How miserable is the mind of the mistaken
    individual! ༔
It apprehends the nonarising phenomena as ego
    and self. ༔
I deeply apologize for this in the nonarising space of
    great bliss. ༔

When the nature of dharmata is not cognized in the
    mind, ༔
One does not understand that appearance and existence
    are illusory ༔
And gives rise to attachment to material things and
    wealth. ༔
I apologize for this in the unattached dharmata of
    nonarising. ༔

Not understanding that samsara is devoid of a self-
    nature, ༔
One apprehends as concrete and labels phenomena to be
    permanent ༔
And, out of unvirtuous karma, fixates on attributes. ༔
I deeply apologize for this in the space of flawless
    enlightenment. ༔

When not realizing the equal nature as being equality, ༔
One apprehends friends and deluded companions to be
    permanent. ༔
How mistaken is this mind of an ignorant person. ༔
I deeply apologize for this in the space of the nature of
    equality. ༔

When not facing the true nature of dharmata, ༔
One abandons the true nature and endeavors in unvirtu-
    ous actions. ༔
Discarding the Buddha's words, one is deceived by mun-
    dane distractions. ༔
I deeply apologize for this in the dharmata space of
    great bliss. ༔

When awareness wisdom is not liberated in itself, ༔
One abandons the self-cognizant nature and endeavors
    in distracted actions. ༔
How pitiful is such a meaningless sentient being! ༔
I deeply apologize for this in the space free from
    approaching or keeping distance. ༔

FROM *The Apology within the Expanse of the View,*
CONTAINED IN THE OLD NYINGMA TANTRAS

The Bodhisattva's Aspiration

Hoh

As all the victorious ones and their sons of the past ៖

Roused their minds toward unexcelled supreme
enlightenment, ៖

I too will accomplish buddhahood ៖

In order to benefit my mothers, all beings as numerous
as space is vast. ៖

PADMASAMBHAVA,
Barchey Künsel REVELATIONS

The Karma of Giving

Compassionate Buddha, I supplicate you—
Look upon us, your followers!

I shall now sing of the benefit of virtue:
Listen to me with a joyous, undistracted mind!

If you offer even a single flower or incense stick
To the Three Jewels, you will be reborn in the Immutable
    Buddhafield.

If you offer butter lamps, in your next life you will have
    a beautiful appearance
And obtain the clairvoyance of celestial beings.

If you offer service to the sangha,
In your future lives you will be a great king.

If you offer fields and crops,
You will enjoy the increasing bliss of the higher realms
    and pure lands.

If you serve your parents, you will never be disparaged,
And in your next life you will surely go to the higher
    realms.

If you give food, you will have a beautiful complexion
and a long life,
And you will be gifted with great strength and enjoy
abundance of food and wealth.

If you give drink, you will have all your sense faculties
intact,
And, when thirsty, you will find something delicious to
drink.

If you give clothes, you will have a beautiful appearance
and fine complexion,
And will have good clothing in all of your lives.

If you give a horse, you will achieve the four bases of
miraculous powers
And will be able to go wherever you wish.

If you give a cow, you will have strength and fine color
And a great abundance of milk, curd, butter, and other
riches.

If you give food to a large anthill,
You will be reborn as the king of a vast country.

If you give the Dharma, you will obtain clairvoyance;
You will remember your former births and swiftly attain
buddhahood.

If you repair a boat, a path, or a bridge,

From life to life you will go from bliss to bliss and be
    respected by all.

If you erect sacred objects related to the body, speech,
    and mind,
Your life span and merit will increase;
In the present, you will be happy,
And ultimately you will attain buddhahood.

If you offer prostrations and circumambulations,
You will be reborn as a universal monarch
As many times as the number of dust particles beneath
    your prostrate body.

If you recite the *mani*,[12]
You will be free from sickness and will remember your
    former lives;
At death you will be reborn in Sukhavati.

If you have great compassion, you will have a long life,
    progress in the Dharma,
And, not remaining in the peace of nirvana,
Become a guide for beings.

May all men and women who hear this song
Practice virtue and swiftly attain buddhahood.

LAMA SHABKAR, FROM HIS AUTOBIOGRAPHY

The Vajrayana Perspective

HUNG

The Three Roots of the bodhichitta of natural
awareness ॰

Do not exist anywhere but in the state indivisible from
myself. ॰

Within it, all the mandalas of victorious ones are
complete. ॰

I naturally confirm this in the primordially uncontrived
state. ॰

OM AH HUNG GURU DEVA DAKINI SARVA SAMAYA
SATVAM BODHICITTA JNANA AH

PADMASAMBHAVA,
Barchey Künsel REVELATIONS

Phowa Supplication

Emaho

Most wonderful lord Amitabha,

Great Compassionate One, and Vajrapani, achiever of
   great strength,

I supplicate you with one-pointed mind;

Grant your blessings to master the profound path of
   phowa.

When I and others arrive at the time of death,

Grant your blessings that my mind may transfer to
   Sukhavati.

NAMCHÖ MINGYUR DORJE, FROM
HIS TERMA REVELATIONS

Parting from the Four Attachments

The one attached to this life is not a practitioner.
The one attached to samsaric existence has no
    renunciation.
The one attached to selfish aims has no bodhichitta.
The one who has any attachment at all does not have the
    view.

MANJUSHRI, IN A VISION TO SAKYA PANDITA

Emptiness and Dependent Origination

The nature of samsara and nirvana lacks even an atom of
   existence.
The dependent origination of cause and effect is
   unfailing.
These two are mutually without conflict; in fact, they are
   a support for one another.
May we realize the intent of Nagarjuna.

TSONGKHAPA

Seeing the Nature of Mind

Resting the watcher in awareness, there is a vivid
    emptiness,
Colorless and devoid of material substance.
Not forming the thought "It is empty!"
That is the moment of seeing the nature of mind.

CHOKGYUR LINGPA

The Eleven Signs of a Sublime Personage

It is a sign of a sublime personage to be less envious and conceited.

It is a sign of a sublime personage to have less craving and be content with just the basics of living.

It is a sign of a sublime personage not to be pompous, haughty, or arrogant.

It is a sign of a sublime personage to be without hypocrisy or double-dealing.

It is a sign of a sublime personage to examine precisely and conscientiously any course of action and then carry it out with mindfulness.

It is a sign of a sublime personage to be on guard concerning the karmic consequences of actions, as carefully as he would protect his own eyes.

It is a sign of a sublime personage to be free from duplicity in keeping vows and samaya commitments.

It is a sign of a sublime personage not to be prejudiced or false-hearted toward sentient beings.

It is a sign of a sublime personage to be forgiving and unaggressive toward those who do evil.

It is a sign of a sublime personage to offer all victories to others and accept all defeats for himself.

It is a sign of a sublime personage to differ from worldly-minded people in all thoughts and deeds.

These were the eleven signs of a sublime personage. Their opposites are the signs of not being a sublime personage.

GAMPOPA,
Precious Garland

Early Dzogchen Masters

At the time when the general vehicles were being taught, Garab Dorje emanated from Shri Vajrasattva's heart, went before the five hundred panditas living in the lands of India, and said:

"I have a teaching that is superior to your eight vehicles, more wonderful than the unified view of Mahamudra; a teaching for awakening if realized in the morning or awakening if realized at night; that is the essence of all views, the realization of all buddhas, the summit of all vehicles, the true and ultimate teaching. It is known as the sacred Great Perfection."

The five hundred panditas did not comprehend this, but rather, they arranged a time for a debate. At the Vajra Throne they debated the nine gradual vehicles for three months.

Ati is the Indian word. In Tibetan it stands for "nonarising self-existence." *Yoga* has the meaning of training in "connecting with the real." When debating on this vehicle, the five hundred panditas were headed by the master Manjushrimitra. Manjushrimitra said:

"You other panditas will not be able to best him now in a debate on the view. Let me debate. If I win the debate, you shall pierce his tongue and expel him, since he is an incarnation of Mara. If he wins, I shall not be able to bear having denigrated the teaching of the unexcelled fruition, so as apology you shall cut off my tongue with a razor right before him. All of you must then embrace his doctrine."

After having supplicated the Three Jewels, they entered the debate, and Garab Dorje won. The master Manjushrimitra then offered an apology in these words:

Not understanding the view to be the vast innate nature,
I declared experience and emptiness to be nondual, yet
    was bound by clinging.
For this I apologize in the self-existing Great Perfection.

Not understanding the meditation to be free from
    reference point,
I went astray, mentally contriving to accept and reject.
For this I apologize in the state of self-manifest
    awareness.

Not understanding the conduct to be free from
    attachment,
I was bound by the clinging of wanting to accept and
    reject on the path.
For this I apologize in unattached yogic conduct.

Not understanding the fruition to be the ground itself,
I sought to find the jewel-like essence of qualities
    outside.
For this I apologize in intrinsically perfect wakefulness.

Not understanding that Garab Dorje is a
    nirmanakaya,

I contested you, seeing you as a non-Buddhist demon.
For this I apologize in the indivisible state of the three
     kayas.

Saying this, he lifted the razor to his tongue, but Garab
Dorje took hold of the razor and threw it away. Then he
spoke:

Manjushrimitra, do not cut off your tongue.
Instead you should uphold my teachings.
Besides having clarified the view,
You have not disputed the meaning of Dzogchen.
Now continue to train in the nature of Dzogchen,
And you will be free from any fault of karmic
     ripening.

GARAB DORJE AND MANJUSHRIMITRA,
Wellsprings of Perfection

Dedication of Merit

By this virtue may all beings, the sentient creatures filling
space,
Be free from misdeeds, faults, and tendencies created
since beginningless time,
And from their deluded imputing, without remainders.
May they recognize their natural face, which pervades all
of basic space.

RANGJUNG RIGPEY DORJE, THE SIXTEENTH
KARMAPA

The Source of Everything

The nature of your mind, groundless and rootless,
Is the basis of all phenomena.

Guhyagarbha Tantra

This single mind is the seed of everything.
From it, samsaric existence and nirvana manifest.

SARAHA, GREAT INDIAN MASTER

Buddhas and Sentient Beings

Covered by the web of disturbing emotions,
One is a "sentient being."
Freed from disturbing emotions,
One is called a "buddha."

NAGARJUNA

Methods of Realization

This intrinsic wakefulness, beyond description,
Is recognized only through the practices of gathering
   accumulations and purifying one's veils,
And through the blessings of a realized master.
Know that depending on other means is but delusion.

FROM *The Great Pacifying River Tantra*

Verse of Auspiciousness

May there be the auspiciousness of true awakening ॰
Indivisible from the spontaneous wakefulness, ॰
The permanent and firm vajra abode ॰
Of the changeless innate nature. ॰

PADMASAMBHAVA

Liberation through Hearing in the Bardo

Verses on the Bardo from the Six Wonderful Methods for Enlightenment Without Cultivation.

Here I shall explain the profound meaning of liberation through hearing for the one who has reached the time of death. Among the three kinds of bardos, the first is the bardo of the time of dying.

Fortunate one of noble family, listen one-pointedly with mindfulness and no distraction. Whatever appears in this world is the dreamlike deception of Mara. Everything impermanent is subject to death. Noble one, abandon suffering!

The experiences of whiteness, redness, and blackness are all the magical display of your mind. These appearances are nothing other than yourself. Don't be afraid or shocked.

Now it seems that you are losing consciousness. Outer appearances resemble the sky at dawn. Inner experience resembles a butter lamp in a vase. Remain one-pointedly in the clarity of nonthought. This luminosity of death is buddha mind itself. Rest naturally without fabricating or distorting anything. Noble one, in this way you will be liberated into dharmakaya.

Give this advice in a pleasant and clear manner. Those of the highest capacity will be liberated through this. Now comes the second bardo of dharmata.

Fortunate one of noble family, listen with undistracted, one-pointed mindfulness. Earlier, you did not recognize awareness. For the next seven days, all experiences will arise as rainbows, lights, rays, spheres, and the bodies of deities. All are the magical display of the means and knowledge of the five buddhas. Do not be afraid or terrified by the brilliant colors and lights. Resolve that they are your own expressions.

Together with these lights, dull colored lights will also appear and attract your mind. Do not be attached to them. They are the self-display of the five poisonous emotions, the pathways of samsara. Your experience will arise as pure and impure paths, so do not miss the right path to be chosen.

From the heart centers of the male and female buddhas of the five families, shafts of light will reach your eyes. This is the great, direct path of Vajrasattva. Quietly abide in awareness and pray, "Look upon me with compassion!" Supplicate with intense yearning. Without accepting or rejecting, without sending away or holding on to anything, maintain the state in which the appearances of deities are inseparable from yourself. At that time, as one deity dissolves into another, you will be liberated into sambhogakaya.

Listen, fortunate one! If you are not liberated now, know that time does not change though phenomena do. Everywhere in the four cardinal and four intermediate directions, above, and below, amid a roaring mass of flames and rainbow colors, is the Great and Glorious Heruka. His assembly of deities and terrifying attendants rain down sharp weapons, HUNG, PHAT, and laughter. This fiery spectacle of immense variety makes the one billion world systems tremble.

Without being afraid or terrified, recognize everything as the display of your awareness. Be firm in this and rest while mingling inseparably with the natural state. Having entered the path, you will be liberated.

In this way, those of the middle capacity are liberated. Third, during the bardo of becoming, say to the dead person:

Listen, child of noble family. Maintain mindfulness and do not be distracted. Your body is now composed of vital energy and mind. Around it arise the appearances of the bardo of becoming. Knowing you are dead, you long to be alive. You are caught by the fierce servants of the Lord of the Dead. Frightening sounds and steep defiles appear, along with many definite and indefinite signs. All this is the manifestation of your mind, which is ultimately empty like the sky. Space cannot be harmed by space. Therefore, develop unconditioned confidence.

This consecrated substance, burned and offered, is an inexhaustible feast, the food of undefiled liberation through hearing. Partake of it, and, without attachment to being alive, turn with longing to your yidam and master.

To the west of here is the Blissful Realm where Buddha Amitabha dwells. Whoever recalls his name will be born there. You, too, while recalling his name, should make prayers. Generate devotion, thinking, "Care for me, Avalokiteshvara and Guru Rinpoche!" Free of doubt, move with a spontaneous vajra leap. In that buddhafield, within the hollow of a lotus bud, you will be swiftly and miraculously born. Therefore, noble one, with delight and joy give rise to devotion.

Those of the lowest capacity are liberated in this way. If not, now comes the way of liberation once one has passed through to rebirth.

Listen, child of noble family. Since you have not closed the door to the womb, when you see a log, a hollow space, a dark place, a forest, or a palace, abandon desire and clinging.

Make up your mind to be born on the earth and specifically in Tibet[13] in the presence of your teacher.

Visualize your future parents, from a religious family, as Guru Rinpoche and his consort. Abandon desire or anger, and with faith enter the state of composure. Having become a vessel for the profound Dharma, you will swiftly attain wisdom.

Through these gradual instructions, no matter how low one's capacity may be, one will certainly be liberated within seven rebirths.

Draw the session to a close with the dedication and aspiration prayers and rest in the natural state of the pure nature of all phenomena.

A deeply profound instruction such as this does not require cultivation but liberates through hearing.

PADMASAMBHAVA,
Essence Manual of Oral Instructions

Undistracted Nonmeditation

The meditation of all beings is spoiled by effort.
While there is nothing at all to be meditated upon,
One should also not be distracted for even an instant.
This, I proclaim, is the meditation of Mahamudra.

SARAHA, GREAT INDIAN MASTER

Mahamudra Aspiration

By learning the scriptures and through reasoning, we are
   freed from the veil of ignorance.
Through contemplating the oral instructions, we
   overcome the darkness of doubt.
With the light resulting from meditation, we illuminate
   the natural state as it is.
May the light of this threefold knowledge increase.

When looking again and again into the unseen mind,
The fact that there is nothing to see is vividly seen as
   it is.
Cutting through doubts about its nature being existent
   or nonexistent,
May we unmistakenly recognize our own essence.

The play of overwhelming compassion being
   unobstructed,
In the moment of love the empty essence nakedly dawns.
May we constantly practice, day and night,
This supreme path of unity, devoid of errors.

RANGJUNG DORJE, THE THIRD KARMAPA,
EXCERPTS FROM *Mahamudra Aspiration of True Meaning*

Ultimate Aspiration

Without fabrication, may I recognize my natural face, in
　itself,
And resolve that all phenomena are the expression of
　this nature!
Gaining confidence in my mind, free from appraising,
May I realize the view of cutting through conceptual
　thinking!

CHOKGYUR LINGPA,
Vajra Bridge

Knowing One Liberates All

The dharmakaya of emptiness is the practice of all accomplished masters. It is the realization of the buddhas of the three times, the life vein of all yidams, the heart blood of all dakinis, the stronghold of all Dharma protectors, the essence of the sutras and tantras, as well as the extract of all the secrecy mantras and knowledge mantras. It is Mahamudra, the Middle Way, and Dzogchen, expounded as one—the pointing-out of dharmakaya as being indivisible from your own mind. It is knowing one that liberates all. It is the single and sufficient king. It is the Mahamudra of reality. It is that which makes one a buddha in the morning when realizing it in the morning, and a buddha at night when realizing it at night. It has great names but also great meaning. Exactly what it is, is to let your own mind, empty and uncontrived, be naturally settled in whatever takes place.

When your mind is restless and thinks of one thing after the other, let your body, speech, and mind rest totally relaxed. In this state, keep a close watch on this busily thinking mind without slipping into distraction.

When it happens that your mind has only slight thought activity, which at times is almost unnoticed, then, resting clear and open, concentrate your mind on being vivid and awake.

When it happens that your mind is dull, obscured, or

drowsy, then rest without feeling attached to the experiences of bliss and clarity. Remain naturally resting without trying to correct anything.

When it happens that your mind is either happy or sad, then rest undistractedly in the one who feels happy or sad.

When it happens that you feel excited and joyful or are honored and served, don't fall prey to the "demon of exhilaration" with your feelings soaring high in the sky. Bow your head, keep your feet on the ground, and let your body and mind rest totally at ease.

When it happens that you are sick and suffer, are robbed or your things are stolen, when you are scolded, defamed, or physically abused, have misfortune or are starving, then don't let your head hang low, don't let your complexion pale or your tears drop, but remain happy, smiling, and in good spirits.

PATRUL RINPOCHE

Thirty Aspirations

May the blessings of a master endowed with the lineage enter
the minds of myself and all others.

May we reach the vital point of truly recognizing the mind
nature.

May realization of this mind nature, as it is, grow forth in
our being.

May we be confirmed with fearlessness and the ten powers.

May superficiality wane and interdependence manifest.

May we have the ability to establish all beings on the path of
ripening and liberation.

May we have the power to traverse the paths and levels in a
single sitting.

May we see the truth of the unconditioned nature with the
eye of knowledge.

May virtues grow like leaves and petals.

May fruition ripen like the wish-fulfilling tree.

May our devotion be firm like Mount Sumeru.

May we have certainty free from doubt.

May our karmic potential waken and our aspirations be pure.

May we have an armor free from mundane defilements.

May our practice be free from obstacles, and may we persist
in bearing hardships.

May our channels, energies, and essences be pliable.

May we always have pure intentions.

May our bodhichitta not degenerate.

May we experience the view and meditation of the
    Mahayana teachings.

May our dualistic mind be naturally liberated.

May we be born in a noble family.

May we be accepted by a master endowed with the lineage.

May we train our minds in the three kinds of knowledge.

May we receive the blessings of empowerment.

May we attain vajralike bliss.

May we attain mastery over consciousness, the channels,
    and winds.

May our body attain the form bodies.

May we directly experience dharmakaya.

May we bring to perfection the welfare of others through the
    activity of the nirmanakaya.

PHADAMPA SANGYE

The Secret Crown Seed Tantra
That Is the Only Child of All Buddhas

In the Kalapingka Dzo yogini language: Buddha Gushtha
Dhakha Emana. ❖

In Tibetan: *sangs rgyas thams cad kyi sras gcig po gsang ba cod pan
sa bon gyi rgyud.* ❖

Homage to the expanse of self-existing nature. ❖
The teacher Samantabhadra, with consort, ❖
Spoke this from the natural expanse: ❖

Listen, retinue, self-expressions of the natural state. ❖
This single self-existing wakefulness ❖
Is the only child of all buddhas. ❖
This empty essence performs all deeds. ❖

It is the seed of Samantabhadra. ❖
This is what everything arises from and is freed into. ❖
This self-existing single tantra ❖
Awakens by seeing, hearing, and remembering. ❖

This seed tantra, the only child of the buddhas, is
complete. ❖
Seal, seal, seal. ❖ Seal of Body. ❖ Seal of Speech. ❖ Seal
of Mind. ❖

BUDDHA SAMANTABHADRA; THIS SHORT TANTRA
IS CONSIDERED TO BE LIBERATION THROUGH
HEARING, READING, AND REMEMBERING

The Essence

The nature of mind is primordially the Buddha,
And this mind, beyond arising and ceasing, is like
    the sky.
Once you realize that all things neither arise nor cease,
The training is then to let be in this nature without
    seeking.

Garab Dorje,
Wellsprings of Perfection

Milarepa's Song

Milarepa said to the girl Paltarbum, "If you sincerely wish to practice the Dharma, in my tradition you don't need to change your name. Since one can awaken to buddhahood as either a monk or a lay person, you don't need to shave your hair off or change your dress."

Then he sang this song on meditation guidance in training the mind with four meaningful analogies:

Listen here, lay girl Paltarbum,
Listen well, rich and dedicated maiden.

Take this sky as your example
And train in the meditation state without center or edge.

Take the sun and moon as your example
And train in the meditation state without increase
    or decrease.

Take this mountain as your example
And train in the meditation state without shift
    or change.

Take the great ocean as your example
And train in the meditation state without face or base.

Take your own mind as the meaning
And train in the meditation state without worry or
    doubt

Teaching her the key points of posture and mind, he told her
to practice meditation. The girl had some fine experience and
understanding. In order to clear up her uncertainty and hindrances, she sang these questions:

Please listen, precious Jetsün,
Please hear me, sublime nirmanakaya.

It was easy to meditate like the sky,
But I felt uneasy when training with clouds.
Now please give me advice on training with clouds.

It was easy to meditate like the sun and moon,
But I felt uneasy when training with planets and
    stars.
Now please give me advice on training with planets
    and stars.

It was easy to meditate like the mountain,
But I felt uneasy when training with bushes and
    trees.
Now please give me advice on training with bushes
    and trees.

It was easy to meditate like the ocean,
But I felt uneasy when training with waves.
Now please give me advice on training with waves.

It was easy to meditate with my mind,
But I felt uneasy when training with thoughts.
Now please give me advice on training with
    thoughts

The Jetsün thought, "She has gained the meditation experience," and he was very pleased. In reply to her request, he
then sang this song of clearing hindrances and bringing forth
enhancement:

Listen here, lay girl Paltarbum,
Listen well, rich and dedicated maiden.

It was easy to meditate like the sky,
And the clouds are the sky's magical display,
So let them be as the very state of the sky.

It was easy to meditate like the sun and moon,
And the planets and stars are the sun and moon's
    magical display,
So let them be as the very state of the sun and
    moon.

It was easy to meditate like the mountain,
And the bushes and trees are the mountain's
    magical display,
So let them be as the very state of the mountain.

It was easy to meditate like the ocean,
And the waves are the ocean's magical display,
So let them be as the very state of the ocean.

It was easy to meditate with your mind,
And the thoughts are the mind's magical display,
So let them be as the very state of your mind.

She practiced accordingly and established certainty in the unconditioned nature, the basic state of her mind. Much later, she passed on to the celestial realms in her own body, accompanied by melodious sounds.

FROM THE *Hundred Thousand Songs of Milarepa*

Verses of Auspiciousness

By the blessings of the supreme Buddha, eminent and
    unexcelled,
The victorious sun of truth,
May the harmful foes of maras and obstructors subside,
So that day and night the auspiciousness of constant
    splendor may be present.

By the blessings of the Dharma of the unconditioned
    nature, eminent and unexcelled,
The sacred Dharma's nectar of truth,
May the painful foes of the five poisonous emotions
    subside,
So that day and night the auspiciousness of constant
    splendor may be present.

By the blessings of the Sangha's qualities, blazing in pre-
    cious brilliance,
The truly beneficial deeds of the Conqueror's offspring,
May the flaws of misdeeds be removed, and may good-
    ness increase,
So that day and night the auspiciousness of constant
    splendor may be present.

Enjoyment of the splendor of immortal life,

Intelligence and discerning insight,
Whatever splendor and wealth of samsara and nirvana
    there may be,
May their auspiciousness be spontaneously present.

May merit increase and flourish like the lofty king of
    mountains,
May great fame spread throughout the sky,
May there be long life, good health, and spontaneous
    benefit for others,
And may the auspiciousness of an ocean of eminent
    qualities be present.

May this place have peace and happiness morning and
    night,
May the midday as well be peaceful and happy,
May there be peace and happiness every day and night,
And may the auspiciousness of the Three Jewels be
    present.

Traditional chant

Space and Awareness

Within the inconceivable naked state of dharmadhatu,
Place ineffable awareness undistractedly.
If a thought arises, it arises out of yourself and dissolves
  into yourself.
There is no basic view, meditation, or instruction
  superior to this

VAIROTSANA, GREAT TIBETAN MASTER
AND TRANSLATOR

Liberation

I have taught you the means of liberation.
But exert yourselves, since liberation depends upon
   yourself.

BUDDHA SHAKYAMUNI,
Vinaya Scripture

The Final Words of Gyurme Dorje

May sights, sounds, and awareness in the state of deity,
    mantra, and dharmakaya
Merge boundlessly as the display of kayas and wisdoms
In the profound and secret practice of the great yoga
And be of one taste with the indivisible sphere of
    awakened mind.

TERDAG LINGPA GYURME DORJE;
OFTEN CHANTED BY A CONGREGATION OF
VAJRAYANA PRACTITIONERS JUST BEFORE A
BREAK, TO SERVE AS A REMINDER DURING
OTHER ACTIVITIES

Dedication of Merit

By this virtue may all attain omniscience.
Having defeated the enemy, wrongdoing,
From the stormy waves of birth, old age, sickness,
     and death,
From the ocean of samsara, may I free all beings.

TRADITIONAL CHANT

Glossary

॰ This mark distinguishes all terma texts (composed and hidden by Padmasambhava) and is a symbol to seal and protect them.

AGGREGATES   Five aspects that comprise the physical and mental constituents of a sentient being: physical forms, sensations, conceptions, formations, and consciousnesses.

AKANISHTHA   The highest or most subtle realm of the awakened state.

AMITABHA   The buddha who resides in the pure land Sukhavati. He is red in color, wears monk's robes, and sits in meditation posture.

ASURA   One of the six classes of sentient beings. They live within sight of the gods but are always consumed with envious battle-mentality.

ATI YOGA   The highest of the six tantric vehicles of Tibet's oldest school. *Ati* means both perfect and effortless. It teaches that liberation is attained through growing accustomed to insight into the nature of primordial enlightenment. Often synonymous with Great Perfection.

AVALOKITESHVARA   The bodhisattva of compassion. Often depicted in a white form with four arms.

AWAKENED MIND   The aspiration to attain enlightenment for the sake of all beings. It is a synonym for "bodhichitta."

BARDO   The intermediate state, usually between death and the next rebirth.

BODHICHITTA   The aspiration to attain enlightenment for the sake of all beings.

BODHISATTVA   A practitioner of the Mahayana path who has developed bodhichitta, the aspiration to attain enlightenment to benefit all sentient beings.

BUDDHAFIELD   The pure realm manifested by a fully enlightened buddha. Other beings can aspire to take rebirth there in order to quickly reach enlightenment.

CHANNELS, ENERGIES, AND ESSENCES   The constituents of the vajra body. The channels are the 72,000 *nadis* and the 40 million minor nadis abiding in the body. The winds are the 21,600 *pranas* circulating within the nadis. Connected with them, the essences, which are the white and red *bindus*, permeate. These three aspects are the subtle bases for body, speech, and mind.

COMPLETION STAGE   Usually means to settle within the unfabricated nature of mind.

CONQUERERS   Awakened buddhas, who have defeated all opposing factors.

DAKINI   A spiritual being who fulfills the enlightened activities; a female tantric deity who protects and serves the Buddhist doctrine and practitioners. One of the Three Roots.

DEITY   In the context of "deity, mantra, and samadhi," is the principle that everything we see is insubstantial and therefore indivisible from emptiness. In order to grow accustomed to this fact, the Vajrayana practitioner visualizes the rainbowlike form of the deity.

DEVELOPMENT STAGE   Training in perceiving the world, sounds, and beings as pure and sacred, which means to regard sights, sounds, and thoughts as deity, mantra, and samadhi. Requires empowerment.

DHARMA PROTECTOR   A being who vows to guard the Buddha's teachings and its followers. Dharma protectors can be either virtuous samsaric beings or enlightened buddhas and bodhisattvas.

DHARMA WHEEL Set of teachings given by Buddha Shakya-muni, who taught three such cycles, known as the Three Turn-ings of the Wheel of the Dharma. "To turn the wheel of Dharma" is a poetic way to refer to giving teachings.

DHARMAS Phenomena, mental objects, constituents of experi-ence.

DHARMADHATU The realm of phenomena, our basic nature in which emptiness and dependent origination are indivisible. Often translated as "basic space." It is the field within which all experience unfolds.

DHARMAKAYA The "body" of enlightened qualities. It is the mind-aspect of enlightenment, which is unconstructed, un-formed, unchanging, empty, and awake. Often counted as the first of the three kayas.

DHATU Element or constituent.

DZOGCHEN Also known as "Great Perfection" and "Ati Yoga." The highest teachings of the Nyingma School of the Early Translations. *Compare with* Mahamudra.

EIGHTFOLD NOBLE PATH Eight aspects of the Buddhist path: right view, thought, speech, action, livelihood, effort, mind-fulness, and concentration.

EMAHO An exclamation of wonder and amazement.

EMPOWERMENT A ritual for conferring authorization to prac-tice the Vajrayana teachings. It is the indispensable entry to tantric practice.

FIVE POISONS Hate, desire, closed-mindedness, pride, and envy.

FIVE TOPICS OF KNOWLEDGE Language, dialectics, healing, arts and crafts, and religious philosophy.

FORM BODIES (*rupakaya*) These include the nirmanakaya and the sambhogakaya.

FOUR MIND-CHANGINGS Reflections on: (1) the freedoms and riches comprising the precious human body, which are so difficult to find; (2) impermanence and death; (3) karma, the law of cause and effect; and (4) the sufferings of samsara.

Reflecting on these four topics regarding the facts of life causes one's mind to change direction from mundane, trivial pursuits and instead be oriented toward spiritual practice.

FOUR NOBLE TRUTHS   The truth of suffering, origin, path, and cessation. The four most basic teachings of Buddha Shakyamuni.

FOUR ROOTS   Murder, theft, sexual abuse, and deception.

FREEDOMS AND RICHES   Conditions for being able to practice the sacred Dharma in a human body. They describe the precious human body.

GANDHARVAS   Class of celestial spirits, noted for their musical talents.

GREAT PERFECTION   A translation of *Dzogchen*.

GURU RINPOCHE   Literally, the "Precious Master," who established Buddhism in Tibet in the ninth century. He hid innumerable Dharma treasures throughout Tibet, Nepal, and Bhutan to be revealed by destined disciples in the centuries to come. He is also known under the names Padmasambhava or Padmakara.

GURU YOGA   A practice for receiving inspirational blessings and mingling with the enlightened state of mind. One of the preliminary practices and a prelude for Mahamudra and Dzogchen.

HERUKA   An enlightened wrathful deity; personifies the wakefulness that consumes ignorance and ego-clinging.

HINAYANA   The vehicle focused on contemplation of the four noble truths and the twelve links of dependent origination.

INDIVIDUAL LIBERATION   Sets of precepts for ordained and laypeople; basic code of morality that is the common foundation for all Buddhist practice.

LUMINOSITY   "Free from the darkness of unknowing and endowed with the ability to know." Can refer to "empty luminosity," like a clear open sky, which is the wakeful quality of the nature of mind; or "manifest luminosity," such as five-colored lights, images, deities, and so forth.

MAHAMUDRA Literally, the "Great Seal." A direct practice for realizing our basic nature. This system of teachings is the basic view of Vajrayana training in the Kagyü, Gelug, and Sakya schools. Its quality is a directness and simplicity that allows the practitioner to connect with his or her basic nature of mind, which is indivisible from the awakened state of all buddhas. The training then is a matter of maintaining that state until it becomes an unbroken continuity.

MAHASATTVA Great beings.

MAHASIDDHA Realized tantric practitioner.

MAHAYANA Literally, "Great Vehicle." The way of those who follow the bodhisattva ideal, intent on achieving liberation for the purpose of freeing all beings from the misery of samsara.

MAJOR AND MINOR MARKS The thirty-two major and eighty minor marks of excellence that characterize the perfect physical form of a nirmanakaya or sambhogakaya buddha.

MARA Demon or demonic influence that creates obstacles for practice and enlightenment. For the spiritual practitioner, mara symbolizes one's ego-clinging and preoccupation with worldly concerns.

MEANS AND KNOWLEDGE Buddhahood is attained by uniting these. In Mahayana, they are compassion and emptiness; and in Vajrayana, the stages of development and completion.

MIDDLE WAY The primary view in Buddhism, that reality defies any conceptual limits we may superimpose.

MOUNT SUMERU World axis. The mountain at the center of a world system, ringed by chains of lesser mountains, lakes, continents, and oceans.

NINE GRADUAL VEHICLES The paths and teachings for Shravaka, Pratyekabuddha, Bodhisattva, Kriya, Upa, Yoga, Maha Yoga, Anu Yoga, and Ati Yoga. The first two are Hinayana; the third is Mahayana; the next three are the Three Outer Tantras; and the last three are called the Three Inner Tantras.

NIRVANA   Extinguishing the causes for samsaric existence. The lesser nirvana refers to the liberation from cyclic existence attained by a Hinayana practitioner. For a buddha, nirvana is the great nondwelling state of enlightenment that falls neither into the extreme of samsaric existence nor into the passive state of cessation.

OBSCURATIONS   The veils of negative emotions and dualistic knowing that cover one's buddha nature, preventing the full attainment of enlightenment.

ONE TASTE   The insight into the fact that all phenomena—the contents of experience—are equally illusory and intangible.

PANDITA   Indian title conferred on especially learned masters, scholars, or professors in Buddhist philosophy.

PHOWA   The phowa practice is performed at the final moment in one's life, while exhaling the last breath, with single-minded devotion to Buddha Amitabha and compassion for all sentient beings.

PRAJNAPARAMITA   Transcendent knowledge beyond concepts.

PRELIMINARY PRACTICES (*ngöndro*)   The general outer preliminaries, the "four mind-changings:" (1) reflections on the precious human body, (2) impermanence and death, (3) cause and effect of karma, and (4) the shortcomings of samsaric existence. The special inner preliminaries are the "four times hundred thousand practices" of (1) refuge and bodhichitta, (2) Vajrasattva recitation, (3) mandala offering, and (4) guru yoga. They are preliminary and necessary in the same way as the foundation is for building a house or loosening the soil is for farming.

ROOT GURU   The master who shows the nature of mind.

SADHANA   Practice, especially with a visualized deity such as Buddha Vajrasattva.

SAMADHI   A state of undistracted concentration, which in the context of Vajrayana can refer to either the development stage or the completion stage.

SAMANTABHADRA   The "Ever-excellent One." (1) The primordial dharmakaya buddha. (2) The bodhisattva Samantabhadra, used as the example for the perfection of increasing an offering infinitely.

SAMAYA   Sacred bond or word.

SAMSARA   Cyclic existence. The vicious circle of birth and death and rebirth within the six realms, characterized by suffering, impermanence, and ignorance. This is the state of all ordinary sentient beings who are bound by ignorance and dualistic perception, karma, and disturbing emotions. Samsara also refers to ordinary reality, an endless cycle of frustration and suffering generated as the result of karma.

SANGHA   Spiritual community, especially noble beings, who are no longer under the power of negative emotions.

SECRET MANTRA   Synonymous with Vajrayana or tantric teachings. Secret means both concealed and self-secret. *Mantra* in this context can either mean "eminent, excellent, and praiseworthy" or "that which protects the mind."

SEVEN PRECIOUS SUBSTANCES   Ruby, sapphire, lapis, emerald, diamond, pearl, and coral. Sometimes the list includes gold, silver, and crystal.

SHAMBHALA   A fabulous kingdom of spirituality situated on this planet.

SHRAVAKA   A hearer or listener. Hinayana practitioner of the Buddha's first turning of the Dharma wheel on the four noble truths.

SIDDHI   Special powers or accomplishments. The supreme siddhi is enlightenment.

SIX CLASSES OF SENTIENT BEINGS   Gods, demigods, human beings, animals, hungry ghosts, and hell beings.

SIX COLLECTIONS   The five sense consciousnesses and the mind consciousness. They cover every type of ordinary experience.

SKANDHA   Gathering or aggregation of many parts. *See* aggregates.

STUPA   A dome-shaped monument housing relics of the Buddha or an accomplished master. The shape of the stupa embodies an elaborate symbolism.

SUGATA ESSENCE   Another word for buddha nature, the enlightened essence inherent in sentient beings.

SUKHAVATI   The pure realm of Buddha Amitabha, praised by all buddhas as the easiest realm outside of samsara in which to take rebirth.

SUTRA   (1) A discourse by or inspired by the Buddha. (2) A scripture within the Tripitaka. (3) All exoteric teachings of Buddhism belonging to Hinayana and Mahayana, the causal teachings that regard the path as the cause of enlightenment, as opposed to the esoteric, tantric teachings.

TANTRA   The Vajrayana teachings given by the Buddha in his sambhogakaya form. Can also refer to all the resultant teachings of Vajrayana as a whole.

TATHAGATA   Literally, "thus gone" or "thus come." One of a buddha's traditional titles.

TEN POWERS   Special abilities with which a buddha is endowed.

TEN SPIRITUAL PRACTICES   Copying scriptures, making offerings, giving alms, listening to discourses, memorizing, reading, expounding, reciting, reflecting upon, and training in the meaning of the Dharma.

TERMA   Concealed treasures of various kinds, including texts, ritual objects, and relics.

THERAVADA   The school of Buddhism that predominates in Southeast Asia, tracing its lineage to the early disciples of the Buddha.

THREE KAYAS   Dharmakaya is the first of the three kayas, and is devoid of constructs, like space. It is the "body" of enlightened qualities. Sambhogakaya (the second of the three kayas) means the "body of perfect enjoyment." In the context of the five kayas of fruition, sambhogakaya is the semimanifest form of the buddhas endowed with the five perfections of perfect teacher, retinue, place, teaching, and time, perceptible only to bodhisattvas. Nirmanakaya means "emanation body" or "form of magical apparition" and is the third of the three kayas. This is the aspect of enlightenment that can be perceived by ordinary beings.

THREE KINDS OF KNOWLEDGE   The understanding and insights we gain when hearing teachings, reflecting on them and applying them in practice.

THREE LOWER REALMS   The worlds of hell beings, hungry ghosts, and animals.

THREE PRECEPTS   The Hinayana vows of individual liberation, the Mahayana trainings of a bodhisattva, and the Vajrayana samayas of a knowledge-holder, a tantric practitioner.

THREE REALMS OF SAMSARA   The realms of desire, form, and formlessness. They cover every possibility of samsaric existence.

THREE ROOTS   Guru, yidam, and dakini. The guru is the root of blessings, the yidam of accomplishment, and the dakini of activity.

THREE SPHERES   Three concepts of subject, object, and action. For instance, while meditating, the mind may maintain the notions of meditator, meditation object, and the act of meditating.

TRIPITAKA   The three collections of Buddha Shakyamuni's teachings: Vinaya, Sutra, and Abhidharma. Their purpose is the development of the three trainings of discipline, concentration, and discriminating knowledge, while their function is to remedy the three poisons of desire, anger, and delusion. The Tibetan version of the Tripitaka fills more than one hundred large volumes, each with more than six hundred large pages. In a wider sense all of the Dharma, both sutra and tantra, is contained within the three collections and three trainings.

TWO ACCUMULATIONS   The accumulations of merit and wisdom.

TWOFOLD AWAKENED MIND The aspiring resolve and the applied resolve.

TWOFOLD BODHICHITTA The aspiring resolve and the applied resolve. The aspiration to attain enlightenment for the benefit of all sentient beings includes loving-kindness, compassion, sympathetic joy, and impartiality, while the application consists of the six paramitas.

VAJRA Literally, "diamond," or "king of stones." As an adjective (i.e., vajra body, vajra speech, or vajra mind) it means indestructible, invincible, firm, and so forth. The conventional vajra is the ritual implement of material substance; the ultimate vajra is emptiness.

VAJRA MASTER A tantric master adept in the rituals and meaning of Vajrayana. The master from whom one receives tantric teaching and empowerment. Can also mean the master who presides over a tantric ritual.

VAJRADHARA Literally, "vajra-holder." The dharmakaya buddha. Can also refer to one's personal teacher of Vajrayana or to the all-embracing buddha nature.

VAJRASATTVA The buddha of purification who embodies all buddhas.

VAJRAYANA The "vajra vehicle." The practices of taking the result as the path. *See also* Secret Mantra *and* tantra.

VICTORIOUS ONE(S) Buddhas and tathagatas.

YIDAM DEITY The buddha in a visualized form.

Contributors

ARYADEVA One of the important Buddhist philosophers of India and a disciple of Nagarjuna, whose writings he explained extensively.

ATISHA Eleventh-century Indian pandita from Vikramashila who spent the last twelve years of his life in Tibet. Founding forefather of the Kadampa School of Tibetan Buddhism, he is also known as Dipamkara Shrijnana.

BARAWA (1310–1391) Early Kagyü master of the Drukpa school.

BUDDHA SAMANTABHADRA The primordially enlightened state of buddhahood from which all other buddhas of the peaceful and wrathful mandalas emanate. This buddha principle is the ultimate source of all the tantras of Vajrayana.

BUDDHA SHAKYAMUNI Literally, "the Sage of the Shakyas," Buddha Shakyamuni is our historical buddha. He was born in Lumbini near the foothill of the Himalayas in what is now Nepal, attained enlightenment in Bodhgaya, turned the wheel of the Dharma in Sarnath, and passed away in Kushinagar. For a detailed account of his life, please read *Lalitavistara*, published by Dharma Publishing.

CHOKGYUR LINGPA (1829–1870) A visionary and revealer of hidden treasures. Regarded as one of the major *tertöns* in Tibetan history, his treasures are widely practiced by both the Kagyü and Nyingma schools. For more details see *The Life and Teachings of Chokgyur Lingpa*, published by Rangjung Yeshe Publications. Chokgyur Lingpa means "Sanctuary of Eminence."

CHÖKYI NYIMA RINPOCHE (1952–) The oldest son of the late Dzogchen master Tulku Urgyen Rinpoche, and the author of *Union of Mahamudra and Dzogchen* and *Present Fresh Wakefulness*, both published by Rangjung Yeshe Publications. He is the abbot of one of the largest Buddhist monasteries in Nepal, located at the sacred Boudhanath Stupa in Kathmandu, Nepal.

DAGNYIMA   Indian female master in the early Dzogchen lineage.

DAKPO TASHI NAMGYAL (1513–1587)   Important master in the Kagyü lineage.

DIGNAGA   Fifth-century author of *Abhidharma Kosha*. Disciple of Vasubandhu, famed for his contributions to pramana, logic, and epistemology. Counted among the most important Indian masters for valid cognition.

DILGO KHYENTSE RINPOCHE (1910–1991)   Regarded by followers of all four schools as one of the foremost masters of Tibetan Buddhism. His collected works fill numerous volumes.

DRIKUNG KYOBPA (1143–1217)   A great master in the early Drigung Kagyu lineage.

DRUBWANG TSOKNYI (1849–1904)   A great master of the Nangchen province in East Tibet. His two main gurus were Chogyal Dorje, a yogi who could fly, and Chokgyur Lingpa. Under his supervision were more than five hundred nunneries.

DÜSUM KHYENPA (1110–1193)   The first Karmapa. One of the main disciples of Gampopa.

DZONGSAR KHYENTSE CHÖKYI LODRÖ (1893/6–1959)   A great master upholding the Rimey (nonsectarian) tradition, as well as being one of the two main root gurus of Dilgo Khyentse.

GAMPOPA (1079–1153)   Foremost disciple of Milarepa and known for writing *The Jewel Ornament of Liberation*. At the age of thirty-two he met Jetsün Milarepa. Among his main disciples were the first Karmapa Düsum Khyenpa and Phagmo Drubpa.

GARAB DORJE (SKT. *Surati Vajra, Prahevajra, Pramoda Vajra*)   Immaculately conceived to the daughter of the king of Uddiyana. He received all the tantras, scriptures, and oral instructions of Dzogchen from Buddha Vajrasattva in person and became the first human master in the Dzogchen lineage. Having reached complete enlightenment, he transmitted the teachings to his retinue of exceptional beings. Manjushrimitra is regarded as his chief disciple. Padmasambhava is also known to have received the transmission of the Dzogchen tantras directly from Garab Dorje's wisdom form. Garab Dorje means "Indestructible joy."

JAMGÖN KONGTRÜL THE GREAT (1813–1899) Also known as Lodrö Thaye. He was one of the most prominent Buddhist masters in the nineteenth century and placed special focus upon a nonsectarian attitude. Renowned as an accomplished master, scholar, and writer, he authored more than one hundred volumes of scriptures. The most well-known are his *Five Treasuries*, among which are the sixty-three volumes of the *Rinchen Terdzö*, the terma literature of the one hundred great tertöns.

JAMGÖN MIPHAM RINPOCHE (1846–1912) A student of Jamgön Kongtrül, Jamyang Khyentse Wangpo, and Paltrul Rinpoche. Blessed by Manjushri, he became one of the greatest scholars of his time. His collected works fill more than thirty volumes. His chief disciple was Shechen Gyaltsab Pema Namgyal. Mipham was regarded as a direct emanation of Manjushri.

JAMYANG KHYENTSE WANGPO (1820–1892) He became the master and teacher of all the Buddhist schools of Tibet and the founder of the Rimey movement. There are ten volumes of his works in addition to his termas. Jamyang means "Manjushri, gentle melodiousness," Khyentse Wangpo means "Lord of loving wisdom."

JIGDREL YESHE DORJE, DUDJOM RINPOCHE (1904–1987) The reincarnation of the great treasure revealer Dudjom Lingpa. He was the supreme head of the Nyingma lineage after exile from Tibet, and many regard him as one of the most prominent scholars and enlightened masters of our time.

JIGMEY LINGPA (1729–1798) The great master of the *Nyingtig* tradition, who had three visions of Longchenpa and received his direct lineage, known as the *Longchen Nyingtig*. He collected and organized the Nyingma tantras. Among his immediate reincarnations are counted Jamyang Khyentse Wangpo, Paltrul Rinpoche, and Do Khyentse Yeshe Dorje.

KARMA CHAGMEY (1613–1678)   A great master of both the Nyingma and Kagyu traditions. His many writings include instructions for retreat practice.

KHAKYAB DORJE (1871–1922)   The fifteenth Karmapa. For his
biography, see *The History of the Karmapas*, published by Prajna
Press.

KYABJE DUDJOM RINPOCHE   *See* Jigdrel Yeshe Dorje.

LONGCHEN RABJAM (1308–1363)   A major lineage master and
writer of the Nyingma lineage. He is regarded as the most important writer on Dzogchen teachings. His works include the
Seven Great Treasuries, the *Three Trilogies,* and his commentaries in
the *Nyingthig Yabshi*. A more detailed account of his life and teachings is found in *Buddha Mind* by Tulku Thondup Rinpoche, published by Snow Lion.

LOREPA (1187–1250)   A great master of the Drukpa Kagyü
school.

MACHIG LABDRÖN (1031–1129)   The great female master who
set down the Chö practice, cutting through ego-clinging. Disciple and consort of the Indian master Phadampa Sangye.
Machig Labdrön means "Only Mother Lamp of Dharma."

MAITREYA   "The Loving One." The bodhisattva regent of Buddha Shakyamuni, presently residing in the Tushita heaven until
becoming the fifth buddha of this eon.

MANJUSHRI   One of the eight main bodhisattva disciples of
Buddha Shakyamuni. He is the personification of the perfection of transcendent knowledge.

MANJUSHRIMITRA   An Indian master of the Dzogchen lineage
and disciple of Garab Dorje.

MILAREPA (1040–1123)   One of the most famous yogis and
poets in Tibetan religious history. Much of the teachings of the
Karma Kagyü schools passed through him. For more details
read *The Life of Milarepa* and *The Hundred Thousand Songs of Milarepa*,
both from Shambhala Publications.

NAGARJUNA   Great Indian scholar at Nalanda university and founder of the Madhyamika school of Buddhist philosophy.

NAMCHÖ MINGYUR DORJE (1645–1667)   Member of the Namchö tradition. Revealer of treasure teachings.

NAROPA   The great mahasiddha of India, chief disciple of Tilopa and the guru of Marpa in the Kagyü Lineage. For more information see *Rain of Wisdom* and *The Life of Marpa*, published by Shambhala Publications.

ORGYENPA (1230–1309)   A disciple of Gyalwa Götsangpa Gönpo Dorje and Karma Pakshi, the second Karmapa (1204–1283). He travelled to the terrestrial pure land Uddiyana where he met the female buddha Vajra Varahi, who transmitted special teachings to him. Teacher of the third Karmapa, Rangjung Dorje.

PADMASAMBHAVA   The miraculous great master who brought Vajrayana to Tibet in the eighth century. He is also referred to as Guru Rinpoche, the precious teacher. For his biography, please read *The Lotus-Born*, published by Shambhala Publications; and *Life & Times of Padmasambhava*, published by Snow Lion.

PATRUL RINPOCHE   A great nonsectarian Tibetan master of the nineteenth century and one of the foremost scholars of his time. He was known not only for his scholarship and learning, but also for his example of renunciation and compassion. His most famous works include *The Words of My Perfect Teacher* and his commentary on *Three Words Striking the Vital Point (Tsigsum Nedeg)*, the epitome of the Dzogchen teachings.

PENGARWA JAMPAL SANGPO   An early master in the Kagyü lineage.

PHADAMPA SANGYE   A great Indian siddha who visited Tibet five times, the last time in 1098, where he taught the Shije system. His chief Tibetan disciple was the yogini Machig Labdron.

PUNDARIKA   The second king of Shambhala.

RANGJUNG DORJE (1284–1334)   The third holder of the title "*Karmapa*," he was a great siddha and scholar and a propagator of both the Mahamudra and Dzogchen teachings to such an extent that he is also counted among the lineage gurus in the Nyingma tradition.

RANGJUNG RIGPEY DORJE (1924–1981) The sixteenth Karmapa. Founder of Rumtek Monastery in Sikkim and countless Dharma centers around the world.

SAKYA PANDITA (1182–1251) One of the Five Sakya Forefathers. He also exercised political power in Tibet on behalf of the Mongols.

SARAHA One of the great siddhas of India and a master in the Mahamudra lineage. He is well-known for his three cycles of spiritual songs.

LAMA SHABKAR (1781–1851) Literally, "White Feet." The name Tsogdruk Rangdrol was given to him because wherever he placed his feet the area became "white" or virtuous. His autobiography, *The Life of Shabkar*, is a must-read.

SHANTARAKSHITA (EIGHTH CENTURY) "Guardian of Peace." The Indian scholar and abbot of Vikramashila and of Samye who ordained the first Tibetan monks. He is the founder of a philosophical school combining the Middle Way and Mind Only. This tradition was reestablished and clarified by Mipham Rinpoche in his commentary on the *Ornament of the Middle Way*.

SHANTIDEVA A seventh-century master at Nalanda monastic university in India. He is regarded as one of the Eighty-four Siddhas. Author of the *Bodhicharyavatara*, published in English as *The Way of the Bodhisattva* by Shambhala Publications.

SHAVARIPA A great Indian master and the guru of Saraha.

SHRI SINGHA (EIGHTH CENTURY) The chief disciple and successor of Manjushrimitra in the lineage of the Dzogchen teachings. He was born in the city of Shokyam in Khotan and studied with the masters Hatibhala and Bhelakirti. Among Shri Singha's disciples were four outstanding masters: Jnanasutra, Vimalamitra, Padmasambhava, and the Tibetan translator Vairotsana.

SONGTSEN GAMPO   The king of Tibet in the seventh century who prepared the way for transmission of the teachings. He is regarded as an incarnation of Avalokiteshvara. He married Bhrikuti of Nepal and Wen Cheng of China, each of whom brought a sacred statue of Buddha Shakyamuni to Lhasa. Songtsen Gampo built the first Buddhist temples in Tibet, established a code of laws based on spiritual principles, and had his minister Thönmi Sambhota develop the Tibetan script. During his reign the translation of Buddhist texts into Tibetan began.

TERDAG LINGPA GYURME DORJE (1646–1714)   Outstanding Nyingma master who built Mindrolling in central Tibet, one of the most important Nyingma monasteries.

TILOPA (988–1069)   Indian mahasiddha, the teacher of Naropa and forefather of the Kagyü lineage in Tibet.

TRISONG DEUTSEN (790–844)   The second great Dharma king of Tibet who invited Guru Rinpoche, Shantarakshita, Vimalamitra, and many other Buddhist teachers to come and teach in Tibet. Until the age of seventeen he was chiefly engaged in ruling the kingdom. He built Samye, the great monastery and teaching center modeled after Odantapuri in India, and established Buddhism as the state religion of Tibet. During his reign the first monks were ordained. He arranged for scholars and translators to render into Tibetan innumerable sacred texts, and he established many centers for teaching and practice. Among his later incarnations are Nyang Ral Nyima Özer (1124–1192), Guru Chöwang (1212–1270), Jigmey Lingpa (1729–1798), and Jamyang Khyentse Wangpo (1820–1892).

TSELE NATSOK RANGDRÖL (1608–?)   Important master of the Kagyü and Nyingma schools. He is also the author of *Mirror of Mindfulness* and *Lamp of Mahamudra*.

TSIKEY CHOKLING II (TWENTIETH CENTURY)   Reincarnation of Chokgyur Lingpa. He resided at Tsikey monastery and was one of the teachers of Tulku Urgyen Rinpoche.

TSONGKHAPA (1357–1419)   Fifteenth-century outstanding scholar and founder of Gelugpa school.

TULKU URGYEN RINPOCHE (1920–1996)   Famed for his profound meditative realization and for the lucid and humorous style with which he imparted the essence of the Buddhist teachings. His method of teaching was "instruction through one's own experience." Using few words, this way of teaching pointed out the nature of mind, revealing a natural simplicity of wakefulness that enabled the student to actually touch the heart of awakened mind. Author of *Rainbow Painting*.

VAIROTSANA (EIGHTH CENTURY)   The great translator during the reign of King Trisong Deutsen. Among the first seven Tibetan monks, he was sent to India to study with Shri Singha. Along with Padmasambhava and Vimalamitra, he was one of the three main masters to bring the Dzogchen teachings to Tibet.

VIMALAKIRTI   Enlightened master and layperson at the time of Buddha Shakyamuni. A very subtle sutra, in which he instructs the Buddha's chief disciples, is translated into English in several versions.

VIMALAMITRA   An early master in the Dzogchen lineage and disciple of Shri Singha and Jnanasutra. Vimalamitra is regarded as one of the three main forefathers for establishing the Dzogchen teachings in Tibet, in the ninth century.

YESHE TSOGYAL   The chief Tibetan female disciple of Guru Rinpoche, who received almost all the transmissions he passed on in Tibet and later compiled his teachings. For details, see *Lady of the Lotus-born*.

Recommended Reading

Here are my top ten books for the beginner as well as the seasoned Dharma practitioner:

1. Bays, Gwendolyn, trans, *The Voice of the Buddha: The Beauty of Compassion* (Berkeley: Dharma Publishing, 1983) (a translation of the Lalitavistara Sutra).
2. Chang, Garma C. C., trans., *A Treasury of Mahayana Sutras* (University Park, Pa.: Penn State University Press, 1997).
3. Gampopa, *The Jewel Ornament of Liberation: The Wish-Fulfilling Gem of the Noble Teachings*, trans. Khenpo Konchog Gyaltsen Rinpoche (Ithaca, N.Y.: Snow Lion Publications, 1998).
4. Lhalungpa, Lobsang P., trans., *The Life of Milarepa* (New York: Arkana Books, 1995).
5. Namgyal, Dakpo Tashi, *Clarifying the Natural State* (Boudhanath: Rangjung Yeshe Publications, n.d.).
6. Patrul Rinpoche, *The Words of My Perfect Teacher*, trans. Padmakara Translation Group (Boston: Shambhala Publications, 1998).
7. Rabjam, Longchen, *The Precious Treasury of the Basic Space of Phenomena* (Junction City, Calif.: Padma Publishing, 2002).
8. Rangdröl, Tsele Natsok, *The Heart of the Matter* (Boudhanath: Rangjung Yeshe Publications, 1996).
9. Shantideva, *The Way of the Bodhisattva*, trans. Padmakara Translation Group (Boston: Shambhala Publications, 1997).
10. Trungpa, Chögyam, trans., *The Rain of Wisdom* (Boston: Shambhala Publications, 1999).
11. Tsogyal, Yeshe, *The Lotus-Born: The Life Story of Padmasambhava* (Boston: Shambhala Publications, 1993).

12. Urgyen, Tulku, Rinpoche, *Rainbow Painting*, trans. Erik Pema Kunsang (Boudhanath: Rangjung Yeshe Publications, 1995).
13. Richard, Mattthieu, trans., *The Life of Shabkar: The Autobiography of a Tibetan Yogin* (Ithaca, N.Y.: Snow Lion Publications, 2001).

Well, well, there are more than ten good books, and there are even more on my yearly updated list of recommended reading. Please see: www.rangjung.com/recom.htm.

Credits

Notes

1. This is a reference to the six paramitas: generosity, pure ethics, patience, perseverance, concentration, and knowledge.
2. The sutras that belong to Buddha Shakyamuni's final teachings on buddha nature and ultimate reality.
3. These "good roots" include decency, generosity, and faith in true goodness.
4. "Beyond sorrow" is also a term for nirvana.
5. *Shamatha* means "stillness." *Vipashyana* is the insight of seeing clearly. These are the two main qualities cultivated through meditation practice.
6. Kashyapa was one of the chief disciples of Buddha Shakyamuni.
7. Shangpa Kagyü was brought to Tibet by Khyungpo Naljor. Chöyul was propagated by Machig Labdrön, and Shije by Phadampa Sangye. The Nyendrub transmission was spread by the siddha Orgyenpa.
8. Soaking sheepskin in water only makes it more rigid and inflexible.
9. The Mind Section is one of the aspects of the Dzogchen scriptures.
10. The first master in the Dzogchen lineage.
11. In addition to the three kayas, the fourth is the essence body, the unformed awakened state that is the identity of all buddhas.
12. The mantra of Avalokiteshvara: OM MANI PADME HUNG.
13. This revelation was written down 150 years ago. Today the aspiration must be directed at any place where the Vajrayana teachings are available.